American Politics and Political Economy Series
Edited by Benjamin I. Page

COMMON KNOWLEDGE

*News and the Construction of
Political Meaning*

W. RUSSELL NEUMAN,
MARION R. JUST,
ANN N. CRIGLER

The University of Chicago Press
Chicago and London

W. RUSSELL NEUMAN is the Edward R. Murrow Professor of International
Communications at the Fletcher School of Law and Diplomacy, Tufts University.
MARIN R. JUST is professor of political science at Wellesley College. ANN N.
CRIGLER is assistant professor of political science at the University of Southern
California

The University of Chicago Press, Chicago 60637
The University of Chicago Press, Ltd., London
© 1992 by The University of Chicago
All rights reserved. Published 1992
Printed in the United States of America
01 00 99 98 97 96 95 94 93 92   5 4 3 2 1

ISBN (cloth): 0-226-57439-3
ISBN (paper): 0-226-57440-7

Library of Congress Cataloging-in-Publication Data

Neuman, W. Russell.
    Common knowledge : news and the construction of political meaning
  / W. Russell Neuman, Marion R. Just, Ann N. Crigler.
        p.   cm. — (American politics and political economy series)
    Includes bibliographical references and index.
      1. Journalism—Political aspects—Developing countries.   2. Developing
  countries—Politics and government—20th century.   3. Political socialization—
  Developing countries.   4. Developing countries—Social conditions—20th
  century.   I. Just, Marion R.   II. Crigler, Ann N.   III. Title.   IV. Series:
  American politics and political economy.
  PN5648.N38   1992
  302.23'09172'4—dc20   92-5992
                                                                              CIP

For
Sara and David;
Hal; and
Mary Adele and John.

Contents

Figures

Tables

Preface

The researcher, who was sitting on a tree stump, leaned forward and asked the Turkish peasant he was interviewing a probing question: "What is the first thing you would do if you were the President of Turkey?" The interviewee was a young man about thirty years old, articulate but uneducated and currently unemployed. He was dumbfounded by the question. He explained to his intrigued inquisitor that he could not imagine himself in such a strange circumstance and proceeded to invoke God's help to prevent him from ever thinking such a thought again.

This interview fragment from research on communication media and political development in the Middle East turned out to provide an important and enduring contribution to the development of political communications theory. It stimulated Daniel Lerner, the principal investigator of that project, to formulate a theory of political empathy. Empathy is defined as the ability of citizens to relate to and understand events and issues outside their own immediate life space. All the peasant knew and understood in this case study was derived from the young man's immediate surroundings and the traditional culture of his village. He knew very little national or world politics. He had no means to know. There were no radios or newspapers available and only an occasional visitor from other villages. It was simply incomprehensible for this young fellow to understand or try to influence public institutions or policies outside of his immediate life space.

Lerner, writing in the optimistic climate of the 1950s, proposed a solution to the problem of political development in the Third World. Aspiring democracies should encourage literacy programs and the development of independent institutions of mass communications—newspapers, magazines, radio, and television. The Third World should copy the successful model of the first. A rich information environment will stimulate citizens to participate and hold leaders to account. Healthy mass media will lead to growing political empathy. Lerner's advice was enthusiastically received and soon became a central element of research and development efforts in this field.

In retrospect, these proposals and the implicit faith in the power of the media they reflect seem a bit naive. First of all, the development of democratic institutions and practices in the Third World turned out to be a much more complex and frustrating process. Second, and this is a central point we confront in this book, American social scientists need not travel to rural Turkey to confront people who feel out of touch with the critical social issues facing their country. They might do as well to sit down with their neighbors. It is the paradox of mass politics in the United States: despite a 200-year-old tradition of public participation, an intense and virtually uninterrupted barrage of video, audio, and print information on local, national, and world events, one finds a conspicuously large number of citizens with only marginal interest in and information about public affairs.

Political disengagement, of course, is not a universal characteristic of industrialized democracies. Some citizens, especially those with higher levels of education, demonstrate an awareness of and feeling of participation in world events. But in the depth interviews we have conducted in the American Northeast, we are struck by how closely the themes which arise resonate with those Lerner uncovered in the Middle East. People explain that they do not have the energy or interest to follow public affairs very closely. They are puzzled by why they should follow issues over which they have no control. Personal experiences and remembered fragments from the news and entertainment alternatively enlighten and obstruct the effort to make sense of national issues and events. Although none of our respondents invoked God's help to keep them from imagining political alternatives, there is a persistent belief in powerful others and a sense of inexplicable events which lie beyond the comprehension and influence of the average citizen. The attempt to relate the abstractions of national political debate to one's immediate life circumstances is a complex, delicate, subtle, and often frustrating process.

In this book we report on an extensive study of how citizens come to understand and learn about events of the world around them. Lerner's insight is sound as far as it goes. A rich and diverse media environment and a literate public are prerequisites to successful representative democracy. We pick up, in effect, where Lerner left off. In a media-rich environment, how do the media choose to report on and characterize the critical issues facing society? Are each of the media equally successful in communicating this information to the public at large? How do people filter, evaluate, and internalize this information as they attempt to make sense of the hubbub of conflicting comments, abstract statistics, and human interest anecdotes?

In the United States we confront one of the most technologically advanced communications infrastructures, a 100-billion-dollar industry of broadcasters and publishers. There are over 10,000 local newspapers, 10,000 national and local journals and magazines, 10,000 radio stations, 5,000 cable systems, and 1,000 television stations. The great majority of these institutions exercise their capacity to cover news and public affairs issues. Yet, somehow, the system of political communication in the United States appears to be falling far short of its potential.

Only half of those eligible bothered to vote in the 1988 presidential elections. This is part of a steady downward trend, the lowest turnout, in fact, since 1924. Participation in congressional and local elections is even lower. Well over half of the adult population assert that they have little interest in politics and agree with the proposition that "government is too difficult to understand."

The premise of this book is that something is missing in the nexus between the news media and the citizenry. Traditionally, when something is amiss, one of the first tasks is to establish culpability. We believe, however, that a scholarly mission of blame-seeking is ill-conceived and ill-advised. Instead we have begun working with a new theoretical perspective in political communications which we believe offers promise to both scholarship and professional practice. The perspective is associated with the term "constructionism." It will be defined in some detail in the pages ahead. Constructionism might briefly be described as a research perspective which focuses on the subtle interaction between what the mass media convey and how people come to understand the world beyond their immediate life space.

This book is an extension of our ongoing attempt to make sense of the puzzles of political communication and mass participation in modern industrial democracies. On different occasions we have had opportunity to pore over the accumulated election surveys of the last three decades, to conduct extended depth interviews about public affairs, to conduct learning experiments, and systematically to analyze the political content of the mass media (Crigler, 1986, forthcoming; Just and Crigler, 1989; Just, Crigler, and Wallach, 1990; Neuman, 1976, 1982, 1986, 1991a; Neuman and Fryling, 1985). This study represents a special and most welcome opportunity to draw on all of the above techniques as part of a systematically integrated and (we hope) theoretically coherent exploration of what constitutes common knowledge in politics and public affairs.

The study was conducted with the generous support of the Spencer Foundation. We would like to express our appreciation to the foundation's President, the late Lawrence A. Cremin, Vice President Marion M. Faldet, and program staff Sunita A. Parikh. Professor Sidney Verba of Harvard University was most helpful in bringing the foundation's interests in this area to our attention. A special note of appreciation goes to Professor Ithiel de Sola Pool of MIT, who offered thoughtful suggestions early on and whose Research Program on Communications Policy provided the stimulating intellectual environment which brought us together.

We are indebted to a large number of graduate and undergraduate students at MIT, Wellesley, and the University of Southern California who helped with the execution of the study including the depth interviewing, the administration of the experimental series including the preparation of the video and print materials, the coding of the media materials, and the depth interview transcripts as well as data entry and data analysis. We would like to thank Loretta Anania, Deborah Campbell, Sarah Dickinson, Jolene Kiolbassa, Aaron MacPherson, Suzanne C. Neil, Jacqueline O'Connell, and Manoj Shahi, whose efforts in the conduct of the experiments, depth interviews, and content screening were especially helpful. Michelle Maxwell contributed to the media content analysis. Kim Foley and Sharad Shankardass lent their expertise to the preparation of the video materials. Diana Gagnon as a postdoctoral fellow in the Media Lab was especially helpful in the design and execution of the modality research. Shawn O'Donnell, Mark Reynolds, and Steven Schneider provided much appreciated skill and expertise in the data management and analysis stage. We are also grateful for the participation of Amy Epstein, Susan Holmberg, Gail Kosloff, and Lee McKnight. Bryan Reece and Paula Lackie helped with the parallel studies of the visual element in broadcast journalism. Deborah Campbell, Jolene Kiolbassa, and Jacqueline

O'Connell wrote master's theses in association with this project, and their special contributions will be acknowledged in the pages ahead.

We are indebted to a number of colleagues who helped with research administration, including Donald Blackmer, Anne Grazewski, Joann Wleklinski, and Dorothy Shannon in the Political Science Department at MIT, and to Nicholas Negroponte, Robert Greene, Lauren Gallant, and Sean Dillman at the MIT Media Lab. We benefitted greatly from constructively critical readings of draft materials by Daniel Bell, Dennis Davis, William Gamson, Doris Graber, Philip Meyer, and Benjamin Page. Of course, despite such able assistance and counsel, we alone are responsible for the shortcomings which remain.

ONE
Knowledge in Common

In this book we examine how citizens in a democracy come to make sense of the political world around them. The study combines several research techniques, not ordinarily used together, to explore the fragile connection between public and private life that Walter Lippmann characterized as "the world outside and the pictures in our heads."

Lippmann's *Public Opinion,* from which that phrase is drawn, was first published in 1922. The book is still widely read and cited, because the questions he raised about the role of public communication in mass democracy are so fundamental. Lippmann argued that the citizen's political world is, by necessity, a pseudo-environment, created for the most part by the mass media who gather, organize, and filter the events of the day because

> the real environment is altogether too big, too complex and too fleeting for direct acquaintance. We are not equipped to deal with so much subtlety, so much variety, so many permutations and combinations. And although we have to act in that environment, we have to reconstruct it on a simpler model before we can manage with it. (Lippmann, 1965 [1922], p. 11)

Lippmann recognized that reconfiguring the political world into a manageable shape is not a deterministic one-way process of media information and persuasion. On the contrary, the creation of the pictures in our heads is an interaction between the extraordinarily diverse "habits, tastes, capacities, comforts and hopes" of each private citizen and the formal traditions of public and media discourse. This interaction between media messages and what the individual already knows and believes about the world is the focus of our study.

In the 1920s Lippmann's attention centered on how the press and the public confronted the First World War. He examined how the war was reported in the newspapers of the day and wondered what a typical American citizen could be expected to learn from those reports about the complex political, economic, and military events in Europe. Sharing Lippmann's concern for the role of communications in the democratic process, we turn in the 1990s to an expanded media environment and a fresh set of issues. We are concerned with what Americans think about the problems they confront in the last decades of the twentieth century—the threat of nuclear arms, race politics in South Africa, the impact of the stock exchange on the national economy, the scourge of drug addiction, or the epidemic of AIDS. Our study asks what people know about these critical policy debates and how well each of the media—television, newsmagazines, and newspapers—can help them to understand the political "world outside."

We are challenged by a stream of research which finds that what people learn from the news media is so dismally disappointing that the United States has become a "nation at risk." This research tradition follows a familiar pattern that we identify as the facts-and-figures fallacy. The analyst selects a few items routinely reported in the news media which have a certain self-evident importance and proceeds to demonstrate just how few survey respondents are actually familiar with the information. Recently, for example, the Markle Commission on the Media and the Electorate expressed concern about voter competence based in part on the inability of many survey respondents to volunteer the name of the Democratic vice-presidential nominee even in the midst of the campaign. The gloomy conclusion was that such findings signal "a widespread, glacial indifference, given the near-saturation media coverage of the Democratic convention" and "front-page attention" to the candidates (Markle Commission, 1989).

Other kinds of evidence about what people learn from their news encounters is sketchy and conflicting. We know, for example, that the average viewer of the evening news can recall without prompting only about one out of the nineteen news stories covered in a typical newscast, but when the viewer is presented with a list of topics, news recall rises to 50 percent (Neuman, 1976). Studies show that self-reported newspaper reading correlates about .35 with a variety of political information indices, while reported TV news viewing correlates only .08 on average, or in some data, negatively (Robinson and Davis, 1990). In a 1990 national survey, only 14 percent of a sample could identify the democratic Czechoslovakian leader Vaclav Havel, but 70 percent knew how Nicolae Ceausescu died, and 82 percent knew where General Manuel Noriega took refuge during the American invasion of Panama (Times Mirror, 1990a). Clearly learning is not a simple function of exposure. Why Ceausescu and not Havel? In our view, the vagaries of name recognition, even of prominent politicians, is a poor measure of the health of a democracy or even the health of its system of political communication.

The Construction of Common Knowledge

Ours is a different concern. We take as our starting point, what people *do* know about public affairs—the *common knowledge* of mass politics. Much past research in political communication has focused on opinions: people's preferences and predilections about political candidates or controversial issues. Common knowledge, however, refers more broadly to what people think and how they structure their ideas, feelings, and beliefs about political issues.[1] Drawing upon a mixture of survey research, content analysis, in-depth interviews, and experiments on learning, we attempt to provide a methodologically integrated and theoretically coherent picture of what constitutes political common knowledge and how the mass media and the public interact to construct common understandings of "the world outside."

In exploring how citizens learn from the news, we start from the premise that the communication task of journalism is indeed a most difficult enterprise.[2] Political communication does not take place in a classroom. There are no study guides, no grades at the end of the term to motivate attention. People pay attention to whatever catches their interest and actively ignore, reorganize, and interpret the news that comes their way (Zukin and Snyder, 1984; Jensen, 1986; Robinson and Levy, 1986; Gunter, 1987; Swanson, 1987; Dahlgren, 1988; Petty, 1988; Bogart, 1989; Langer, 1989).

Just as the mass audience lacks the motivations and discipline of attentive students, news professionals lack the situational advantages of the classroom teacher. Journalists communicate with an audience they cannot see or hear. It is a one-way conversation. They operate in a professional world inhabited mainly by news sources, public-relations specialists, and other journalists. Their social world is also dominated by social and economic elites (Sigal, 1973; Hess, 1981). It is what

Gamson calls the world of "public discourse" (1992). Even a brief opportunity to talk with members of the mass audience who read and view their stories is predictably rare, a product of happenstance, because two-way conversations with the audience for news has not become a part of journalistic practice (Gans, 1979; Levy, Robinson, and Davis, 1986; Kiolbassa, 1989).

The majority of citizens operate in a world outside the rarefied realm of public discourse. It is a personal world, with an equally pressing set of career and family demands, economic and health problems, personal dreams and aspirations. For brief moments in a citizen's hurried day, there is an intersection of these two worlds. Stepping out of the shower in the morning one might hear an interview with a former hostage on the "Today Show," glance at the front page of the morning newspaper over coffee, hear the headlines on the car radio, or catch some of the evening news after dinner. The interconnection of public and private worlds is often unscheduled, incidental, and haphazard. The evolution of common knowledge is not a simple matter of transferring the content of the news, in whole or even in part, to the public.

Public Discourse and Common Knowledge

For the language of public discourse to be meaningfully interpreted in private life, it requires translation. Take, for example, this typical television news story on the harrowing epidemic of AIDS. CBS anchorman Dan Rather introduces the piece:

> In as stern a message as any yet heard about AIDS, a scientific panel today called for a multi-billion dollar a year campaign against the killer disease. CBS News medical correspondent, Susan Spencer, explains why today's report from the U.S. National Academy of Sciences is bound to draw some unfriendly fire.

The correspondent explains that the panel is calling for a two billion dollar program of education and research over the next five years. She explains that there may be controversy over the proposal to distribute free sterile needles to prevent the spread of AIDS among drug users who share needles. She introduces soundbites from three medical experts; Dr. David Baltimore's from the National Academy of Sciences is typical: "We are quite honestly frightened about the future prospects here and we ask that there be strong leadership." She concludes:

The two billion dollars the Academy cites would cover only education and research, not treatment costs, which it has been estimated will be as high as sixteen billion dollars a year by 1990. The Academy today called that figure conservative. Susan Spencer, CBS News, Washington.

It is a classic news story in form and focus for any of the news media. It is driven by the day's events, official news as delivered by authoritative sources at press conferences (Cohen, 1963; McDougall, 1968; Epstein, 1973; Sigal, 1973; Tuchman, 1978; Gamson, 1984; Lewis, 1984; Manoff and Schudson, 1986; van Dijk, 1988). There is a passing reference to a policy dispute, the proposal about free needles which is "sure to cause an uproar." And there are references to two billion and sixteen billion dollars, figures difficult to comprehend other than that they are very large. The story does not make clear, however, where this vast amount of money is coming from or where it is going.

What would a typical viewer remember from such a news story? Not necessarily a great deal and probably not the names of the agencies or officials, or the dollar amounts cited. This news story represents only a fleeting connection between media discourse and evolving public knowledge of the tragic epidemic. The ephemeral nature of a given news encounter, however, does not mean that individuals are unable to think deeply about the problem of AIDS.

In the depth-interview component of our research, we asked our respondents to describe the main idea of a series of political issues including AIDS (see the Appendix for more detail). Their free-ranging responses offer a dramatic contrast between the media's public discourse and the private conceptions of the mass audience. Few of our respondents volunteered federal epidemiology statistics or projected medical research budgets. But most had a great deal to say, such as one seventy-three-year-old retired businessman. He described the AIDS epidemic in highly emotionally charged and moralistic language. For him, AIDS is intimately tied with issues of religion and public discipline. He associates AIDS with San Francisco, in his view a modern Sodom or Gomorrah. He understands the fundamental medical dynamics of the disease, but his thinking about appropriate policy responses to the crisis is structured by much more than just the medical issues:

Q: How would you explain the issue of AIDS to someone who didn't know anything about it?

A: Well, of course, it depends on who you're talking to. If you're talking just about the disease, I think you can only say that it's something that causes a breakdown within the body, that portion that manufactures whatever you need to resist disease . . . and makes you subject for almost any kind of disease . . . and it can be fatal because you don't have any resistance. So, I think that would perhaps explain fairly well for a laymen . . . But there is another aspect to this and that it's against the law of man. What brought this about, this homosexual lifestyle. That's against the law of man. It's against the law of God.

He goes on to describe the origins of AIDS in the lifestyles of the hippies and gays in "Frisco," which he and his wife had visited briefly on a vacation trip.

They were dirty. They had not just long hair, but dirty, dirty, straggly greasy looking hair and they didn't shave and the girls were just as bad as the guys and the guys were walking, hugging each other like lovers holding hands . . . I would never go back to Frisco after that . . . That's my feeling about it. I don't have that much sympathy for them [those afflicted with AIDS]."

He describes himself as not having any direct contact with drug users or gays or individuals with AIDS, but his conception of AIDS is clearly not dependent solely on media messages and information. He constructs a concept of AIDS from fragments of what he hears and what he already believes. His thinking is schematic, and richly so. He shows little sign of being a prisoner of mass media information, caught in the media's cuing and framing of public issues, even in domains where he has minimal direct experience. He draws heavily on personal experience, conversations with others, and non-news media and rails at the press for missing, as he sees it, the main point of the AIDS epidemic: the decline of American moral and religious life. This man's response shows us clearly that understanding how individuals frame issues in the news is critical to understanding both what will be recalled from the flow of news and how such information influences opinion about what ought to be done to respond to these public issues (Jensen, 1986; Graber, 1988; Gamson, 1992).

To study the dynamic interaction among individuals, with their personal interests, beliefs, and experiences, the issues with their varying degrees of complexity, and the media with their different journalistic traditions, we must draw on a variety of investigative techniques. How much does political sense-making depend on the individual, or on the topic, and how much on the way the information is communicated? In the following chapters we will seek to answer those questions, as well as the broader question of how bits of information gleaned from the news fit into a person's larger framework of understanding important topics of public debate. We will focus on the resonances and disjunctures between public and private discourse about politics and introduce a typology of issue frames used in the media and by the mass citizenry. We will compare how different media— television, newsmagazines, and newspapers—present information to the public. We will concentrate on specific news stories and examine the information people pick out of the formal presentation of news to enrich their conceptualization of public issues.

Before we take up our study, however, we review three research traditions that have shaped the study of political communication: (1) the tradition of media-effects research, (2) the uninformed voter paradigm, which contrasts an ill-informed voter against an idealized model of rational choice, and (3) a recently evolving literature on political cognition in the mass public. Information from these studies can be arrayed according to the degree of audience passivity or activity and the concomitant media responsibility assumed by the researchers. Generally theories on media effects emphasize the persuasive and manipulative powers the media exercise over a relatively uninterested, unknowing, and gullible audience. Research on voter sophistication and knowledge has focused on the low level of knowledge among American voters, a level that results not necessarily from media manipulation as much as from public apathy and disinterest in politics. Research on public choice and political cognition has assumed a more active audience stance. These research approaches help us to move to a new conceptualization of political communication in which the audience is seen as constructing meaning from a rich media environment.

The Research Agenda in Political Communication

Much of the research in this area intimates dissatisfaction with the state of political interest, information, or sophistication of the electorate. The blame for the "nation at risk" divides along a continuum of culpability, anchored by the media at one end and the people at the other. We explore various strands of the literature that focus on the negative impact of "media effects" and the disappointing performance of the uninformed voter. We show how concepts such as the "cost" of information and the "bounded rationality" in which real world political choices are made help us to avoid the endless debates over whether the glass is half-full or half-empty that characterize much of the research on big/little media effects and the oh so/not so uninformed voter. We lean heavily on the contributions of cognitive psychology in developing an approach to political communication that takes account of the construction of news and the citizen's understanding of media messages.

Media Effects Theory

The traditional view of the way citizens gain information from the media is dominated by imagery of a vegetative audience, passively absorbing media influence. In one form or another, many analysts draw on the logic of Plato's famous allegory of the cave.

> Imagine the condition of men living in a sort of cavernous chamber underground with an entrance open to the light and a long passage down into the cave. Here they have been from childhood, chained by the leg and also by the neck so that they cannot move and can see only what is in front of them because the chains will not let them turn their heads. At some distance higher up is the light of a fire burning behind them; and between the prisoners and the fire is a track with a parapet built along it, like the screen at a puppet show, which hides the performers while they show their puppets over the top . . . The prisoners, having seen nothing but shadows, cannot think their words refer to the objects carried past, behind their backs. For them, shadows are the only realities. (Plato, 1945, *The Republic,* book 7)

Plato's allegory compellingly anticipates the mass citizenry dispersed in their private homes, huddled in front of flickering television screens and trying to make sense of the world at large around them. They are at the mercy of the television puppeteers. How could they possibly understand the full complexities of the political debates which are simplified and caricatured for them by professional journalists? How could they know anything of the world except what they are shown? This is, in effect, the theory of media manipulation that has dominated the literature on media effects.

Media manipulation theories. This notion of a helpless audience is both the oldest and most broadly focused paradigm of political communication effects. It arose from the study of propaganda and mass society rooted in the historical period of authoritarian manipulation of public opinion in Europe beginning with the First World War (Kornhauser, 1959; De Fleur and Ball-Rokeach, 1988; Davis, 1990; Neuman, 1991b). More recent research in a critical tradition characterizes the audience as powerless to resist the persistent, pervasive, and emotionally sophisticated persuasions of an interlocking media-political-economic establishment (Marcuse, 1964; Curran, Gurevitch, and Woollacott, 1977; Bagdikian, 1983; Gerbner, 1983; Bennett, 1988; Entman, 1989; Schiller, 1989). Research in this tradition identifies various mechanisms of media manipulation, including agenda-setting, salience cuing, priming effects, issue framing, mainstreaming, and ideological cultivation (Weiss, 1968; McGuire, 1969, 1986; Kraus and Davis, 1976; Comstock et al., 1978; Erbring, Goldenberg, and Miller, 1980; Roberts and Bachen, 1981; Zukin, 1981; Kinder and Sears, 1985; Davis and Robinson, 1989; Davis, 1990; Page and Shapiro, 1992).

The key problematic of this research tradition is somewhat awkwardly poised on a debate over minimal versus large media effects. The bête noir for many effects researchers is Joseph Klapper. His 1960 review of the literature concluded that media messages generally had minimal effects. His work became the jousting dummy for virtually a generation of communications researchers who felt obliged to prove, after all, that the media do indeed have significant effects on their audiences.

The basic methodology for demonstrating effects involves a statistical correlation between the issue agenda, preferences, perspectives, and assumptions of the audience and some corresponding measure of relative emphasis in the media (Clarke and Kline, 1974; Katz, 1980; McLeod and Reeves, 1980; Neuman, 1989; Nimmo and Swanson, 1990). For example, the cultivation analysis school found that those who watch a great deal of television tend to exhibit higher levels of mainstream and stereotypical thinking which could be derived from the simplifying caricature that dominates informational and entertainment television programming (Signorielli and Morgan, 1990).

Agenda-setting researchers found correlations between the amount of media coverage of public policy issues and the importance attached to those issues by survey respondents (McCombs and Shaw, 1972; McCombs, 1981; Weaver et al., 1981; MacKuen, 1984; Protess and McCombs, 1991). Experimentalists found that when the relative emphasis on various issues was subtly altered in television newscasts watched in a laboratory, such alterations affected the subjects' ratings of issue importance, their sense of responsibility for social problems, and their assessments of public figures (Iyengar and Kinder, 1987; Iyengar, 1991).

The television hypothesis. Because so much of the growth of media coverage and public reliance has involved television in recent years, the new messenger has received more than its share of attention from researchers in the media manipulation tradition. The "television hypothesis" is well documented. Book-length studies of political communication focusing on television to the virtual exclusion of the print media are now commonplace (Meyrowitz, 1985; Robinson and Levy, 1986; Gunter, 1987; Iyengar and Kinder, 1987; Kubey and Csikszenthmihalyi, 1990; Quester, 1990). Television, however, is only one of the most recent media to be scrutinized and held accountable for the deterioration of society (Wartella and Reeves, 1985). If possible, the tone of television-centered research is even more critical than the previous run of media manipulation studies. Patterson and McClure condemn television news coverage as "so fleeting and superficial that it is almost meaningless" (Patterson and McClure, 1976, p. 36).

Those who blame television for the deficiencies of public information often argue that twenty-two and a half minutes of nightly news cannot possibly provide an adequate knowledge base for the citizenry. One of the important pieces of evidence here is the survey research data which show that people who claim to rely on television as their primary news source are less informed about public issues than print users. Robinson and Davis, for example, in a recent review of research conclude that "there has been growing evidence that television may be less useful than newspapers or word of mouth at conveying information to the public" (Robinson and Davis, 1990, p. 108). The problem of causal inference is complex, however, and it is not yet clear whether there might be other prior factors that may explain both individuals' reliance on non-print news media and their low level of interest in and knowledge about political life. Nevertheless, television serves as a convenient target of critical research; the growing dependency of the public on television news is being used to explain increasing political alienation, the drop in political participation, a declining role for political parties, and an overall evisceration of political debate (Barber, 1978, 1979; Robinson, 1975, 1976; Ranney, 1983; Arterton et al., 1984; Graber, 1984; Jamieson, 1988; Milburn and McGrail, 1990; Wattenberg, 1991).

The media dependency hypothesis. One component of the media effects tradition of research emphasizes not simply a reliance on television, but rather a dependence on media generally. Citizens have come to depend on the media because they have virtually nowhere else to turn for information about public affairs and for cues on how to frame and interpret that information (Becker and Whitney, 1980; Gerbner et al., 1980; McDonald, 1983; Robinson and Sheehan, 1983; Ball-Rokeach, 1985; Ball-Rokeach et al., 1990). Doris Graber develops the argument by example:

> Just imagine what would happen if all mass media ceased to function and remained inactive for an entire year! No news about events at home and abroad. No explanations about shortages or failures of public services. No announcements of new programs and facilities. Presidents, governors, and mayors, and legislators at all levels would be slowed or immobilized by lack of information and interpretation. And you—how would you fare, relying solely on your own daily experiences and word-of-mouth? Indeed, media are vital for public and private life; the image of a modern world without them is eerie and frightening. (Graber, 1984, p. ix)

Becker and Whitney explain the historical roots of the perspective: "as the social system becomes more complex and the informal channels of communication become disrupted, members of society become more dependent on the mass media. The result is that members of modern urban-industrialized societies are becoming almost totally dependent on the media for even rudimentary pieces of information" (Becker and Whitney, 1980, p. 95).

The media, then, have the potential for significant influence because they are so central to the functioning of society and to the individual's ability to acquire information about wider political and economic aspects of society. The actual learning of information, however, may depend on the individual's motivations, uses, and anticipated rewards of using the media.

The media gratifications approach. Researchers in this evolving tradition argue that media effects depend on the "uses and gratifications" that the audience members use to orient their media experiences (Katz and Lazarsfeld, 1955; Katz, Blumler, and Gurevitch, 1973; Blumler and Katz, 1974; McLeod and Becker, 1981; Rosengren, Wenner, and Palmgreen, 1985; Perse, 1990). So, if one is puzzled by why the stock market crashed in October 1987 and finds more extensive background economic coverage in the newspaper and less, for example, on television, then that individual's needs will more appropriately be met by the newspaper coverage. Here audience members are seen not as simple, passive recipients of media messages, but as people who demand and expect the media to serve particular functions.

The media gratifications tradition has focused more on generalized motivations of media behavior (emphasizing, for example, entertainment versus information) and motivations for use of particular media (books versus television) rather than probing why people are attentive to certain messages and how they use that information (McLeod and Becker, 1981; Blumler, Gurevitch, and Katz, 1985).

The Uninformed Voter

While media effects researchers see the problem in terms of manipulative media facing relatively passive audiences, other researchers concentrate on the stubbornly ignorant and uninterested political audience—the uninformed voter. The key problematic here is the contrast between an idealized model of the citizen, drawn from economic theories of collective choice, and survey evidence of low political sophistication within the potential electorate. How can citizens exercise popular control over elected officials if they are hazy about where the candidates stand on the issues? For this paradigm, however, the problem lies not so much with the failings of the political and media establishment as with the voters themselves.[3]

This research tradition relies for the most part on the results of public opinion surveys. Interestingly, survey-based public opinion research has traditionally done better at measuring opinions than at measuring knowledge. One reason is that survey interviewing techniques are premised on maintaining respondent rapport (Babbie, 1973). Researchers are reluctant to ask questions with generally accepted right or wrong answers which may prove potentially embarrassing. Another reason is that the traditional research paradigm focuses on explaining the correlates of policy preference and vote choice rather than the knowledge base from which such preferences may be derived. In fact, much of the received wisdom about the "uninformed public" is not derived from knowledge-oriented questions at all but is inferred from the modest correlations of voter policy or ideological preferences (as measured by one or another scale) and the individual's placement of candidates and parties on similar scales.

When surveys do focus on knowledge rather than opinion, they tend to be based primarily on rather narrowly conceived questions that one might associate with high school civics, such as the length of senators' terms or a definition of "Electoral College." Using textbookish tests of political knowledge, the classic survey-based voting studies of the 1940s and 1950s established a model of a partially informed voter heavily dependent on party labels and evaluations of candidates' personal qualities rather than issue positions (Berelson, Lazarsfeld, and McPhee, 1954; Campbell et al., 1960, 1966; Converse, 1964). Voters' policy attitudes were found to conform to a pattern of "self-interest in a primitive and short-sighted sense" rather than to any liberal-conservative ideology (Campbell et al., 1960). These studies, like the Klapper volume, became the target for younger researchers who wished to rescue the reputation of the lowly citizenry from the methodological inferences and elitist presumptions of their forebears (Nie, Verba, and Petrocik, 1976; Judd and Milburn 1980; Natchez, 1985).

Like the debate over minimal versus large media effects, the brouhaha over unenlightened voters is awkwardly unresolved. And like the effects debate, there is enough ambiguity in the modest correlations between issue positions and vote choices to fuel endless debate.

The idealized model against which citizens have been invidiously compared derives from the study of public choice, which takes a mathematically oriented and game-theoretic approach to the puzzle of accumulating private preferences into public policy. Most analysts avoid the voter information problem by positing a model in which all voters have well-developed preferences and virtually complete information on relevant candidates and parties. Much of the work in this tradition is non-empirical and purely theoretical, demonstrating, for example, how different voting procedures affect the weighted impact of different minority policy positions in multiparty elections (Elster, 1986). When empirical results are introduced, they draw on aggregate statistics at the macro and institutional levels of analysis, in which most of the micro-level random noise of individual "errors" and decisions based on limited knowledge cancel themselves out (Riker and Ordeshook, 1968; Shepsle, 1972; McKelvey and Ordeshook, 1984). Thus, a typical study concludes that "in principle, it is possible for voters to vote as if they were informed and for the electoral process to be responsive to voter preferences even in very sparse informational environments" (McKelvey and Ordeshook, 1990, p. 311). In the past few years, research in this tradition has expanded empirical testing of the theory and even started to incorporate communications and information variables into public choice modeling (Ferejohn and Kuklinski, 1990).

Our own work picks up on this branch of the public choice model, focusing on the costs and benefits of information acquisition. In his seminal work, Anthony Downs argues that it may be completely rational not to vote at all, or not to collect the information necessary for an informed choice (Downs, 1957). Following that argument, Herbert Simon (1985) calls for an investigation of the information environment of "bounded rationality," real individuals coping with all of the demands of individual and collective life confronting a flood tide of political information. Our study attempts to respond to their invitation as we focus on the motives and behaviors of citizens as they develop ideas about critical issues in the public policy debate.

The Political Cognition Perspective

Our approach to public learning draws on the recent literature on political cognition. The key problematic here is the structure of political thought more than the effect of issue-opinions on the vote. Robert Lane's early work (1962) in this area employed extended depth-interviews with fifteen men of "Eastport" to examine the unique and common structuring of individuals' political ideologies. In a later article (1973), Lane explicitly contrasts his natural-language study of "political reasoning" to the survey-based conclusions of Converse and others on "issue constraint" and concludes that the cognitive approach and its methods by their nature generate a very different picture of the "uninformed voter." More recent investigations in this tradition focus on individual strategies for processing political information in the face of constraints and distractions in other life areas (Graber, 1984). A central concept of political cognition is the notion of schema or simplifying maps of how political facts and figures can be organized into a meaningful whole (Graber, 1984). Lau and Sears (1986), for example, draw together a number of investigations which demonstrate how schematic outlines of candidates and issues are intertwined with the calculation of a vote decision. When individuals do not have enough time and energy fully to survey the political horizon, they may rationally employ some cognitive heuristic to make the task more manageable (Downs, 1957; Converse, 1964; Paivio, 1978; Kahneman, Slovic, and Tversky, 1982; Perloff, Wartella, and Becker, 1982; Conover and Feldman, 1984; Simon, 1985; Lau and Sears, 1986; Bruner, 1990). The key problematic, then, focuses on whether the use of cognitive shortcuts, such as attribution techniques, distorts what would otherwise be a rational political preference.

The study of symbolic and sociotropic politics brings the perspective of political cognition into conflict with the underlying assumptions of rational behavior in the uninformed voter paradigm. There is considerable evidence that emotional responses to political symbols, often developed early in life and persisting through adulthood, influence political choices and the processing and conceptualization of new political information (Edelman, 1964; Lau, Brown, and Sears, 1978; Sears, Hensler, and Speer, 1979; Sears et al., 1980; Sears, 1990; Sears and Funk, 1990). Furthermore, while public choice theory is premised on the strategic expression of self-interest within the electorate, evidence of "pocketbook voting" is surprisingly scarce (Sniderman and Brody, 1977; Schlozman and Verba, 1979; Kinder and Kiewiet, 1981; Kiewiet, 1983; Sears and Lau, 1983; Kinder and Sears, 1985). Although retrospective voting on economic issues is plausible in the aggregate, a closer look at the individual level of how people make sense of the options put before them reveals a diversity of information, strategies, conceptualizations, values, and beliefs.

The Construction of Political Meaning

This review of the issues in the literature of political communication and behavior has been selective and purposeful. Our intent has not been to chronicle research trends but to erect a theoretical platform from which to launch a fresh approach to enduring questions of mass political behavior. We have singled out three themes: media effects, the uninformed voter, and political cognition, critiquing the first two to build on the third.

The first thematic sets up an irresolvable contest between minimal and maximal media effects. Although such an artificial polarity may be a useful classroom technique, it does not admit a definitive answer. Most troubling is the notion of "media effects" itself which, in its less sophisticated formulations, posits a passive and unthinking audience "affected" by media messages of various sorts. We seek a more systematic understanding of the conditions under which some people learn from or are persuaded by messages and images in their media environment. This conditional focus moves away from the mechanistic and deterministic model of media effects.

The second thematic sets up an equally irresolvable tension between a model of the self-interested issue-focused rational citizen-voters and empirical evidence of distracted, half-attentive, and less-than-fully informed real human beings. Controversy surrounds the use of survey and experimental data that attempt to prove "once and for all" that voters are (or are not) fools. We agree with Converse, one of the founding fathers of this tradition, that it is time to leave that debate and turn to the study of underlying questions about how citizens interpret the political issues put before them by politicians and the media[4] (Converse, 1980).

The third stream of research is loosely labeled the cognitive perspective. It starts not from a divisive polarity but a straightforward question—how do people think about politics? Drawing from and expanding the media gratifications tradition, it asks how people use the media to learn what they feel they need to know. In asking what kinds of media and what kinds of messages are likely to attract the citizen's attention, it assumes neither a passive nor an active audience member. The central research question in the field of mass communications and politics need not be a debate over the amount of "effect" of the media on the populace but might well be a more balanced inquiry into the interaction of media, media messages, and public understanding—the study of how people construct meaning from the flow of political discourse around them.

Toward a Constructionist Model of Political Communication

Expanding on Gamson's (1988) early model of the new paradigm, we characterize constructionism as reflecting the following general principles of theory and methodology:

- Constructionism emphasizes the prospect of an active, interpreting, meaning-constructing audience. This is a long-standing impulse of researchers in the field (Kraus and Davis, 1976) but one that has proved frustratingly difficult to achieve in the practice of empirically grounded research (Rosengren, Wenner, and Palmgreen, 1985).
- Constructionism studies the "interaction" between the audience member and the media rather than a narrowly defined "effect" of media on the audience. Delia and O'Keefe (1979), for example, emphasize defining communication as the creation of meaning in interaction rather than in terms of influence. This model of communication as "conversation" provides a particularly attractive model for mass communications researchers.[5] When an individual enters an ongoing conversation, there is an "implicit negotiation of the definition of the situation, an answer to the question, 'What is going on here?'" (Delia and O'Keefe, 1979, p. 179). The same dynamic, we argue, applies to an individual who turns on a television newscast or opens a newspaper.
- Constructionism emphasizes the importance of the varying character of the communications content. Different kinds of issues are interpreted by the media and by the public in different ways, and communications theory must be sensitive to these differences. In many traditional models of attitude change and persuasion, for example, the substance of the message (or issue, in our vocabulary) receives relatively little attention. In Hovland's work, topics were often selected because they were demonstrably unimportant or obscure, thus presumably leaving room for measurable attitude change (Neuman, 1989, p. 216). But the constructionist approach, in contrast, draws attention to the character of the issue, its salience to individuals, and their prior knowledge.
- Constructionism emphasizes the importance of the medium of communication, including the historical, struc-

tural, and technological character of media institutions. Thus the varying journalistic traditions of broadcast and print journalism, evolving public expectations of what each medium does best, and the physical modalities of textual versus audio and audio-video communication are drawn in as explicit variables for analysis (McLuhan, 1964; Worchel, Andreoli, and Eason, 1975; Cohen, 1976; Hirsch, 1977; Gans, 1979; Salomon, 1979; Robinson and Sheehan, 1983; Graber, 1988; Delli Carpini and Williams, 1990; Kosicki and McLeod, 1990).

• Constructionism focuses on "common knowledge" as opposed to "public opinion": what people think and how they think about public issues rather than narrowly defined valence-oriented "opinions" concerning an issue or candidate. The use of "knowledge" rather than "opinion" emphasizes the need to organize information into meaningful structures. The phrase "common knowledge" emphasizes that the structuring and framing of information is not unique to each individual but aggregates into the cultural phenomenon of shared perspectives and issue frames.

• Constructionism is non-evaluative in character. The paradigms of media effects and the uninformed-voter each set up an idealized model of rational citizenship in a rich information environment. When measured against the Madisonian ideal, the voter (and in some cases the media) comes up short. Even when researchers in these traditions testify for the defense, asserting that voters are not fools, they do so within the original paradigm. Constructionist theory turns the original question on its head. One does not start with an idealized model of rational issue-voting and design studies to see if the voter measures up. It focuses on what motivates people to pay attention to some public issues rather than assuming that civic duty simply requires attention to all matters political. One asks, simply, how do people become informed about the political world around them, and how do they use the information they have acquired?[6]

• Constructionism is inherently comparative. This affects both theory and methodological strategy. The Latin derivation of the word *communication* emphasizes "that which is held in common." Thus as analysts we compare how information about different types of issues is organized and structured in the public discourse of different media and focus on how that information compares with public perceptions. This three-way interaction of individual, medium, and issue which characterizes constructionist research is summarized in figure 1.1.

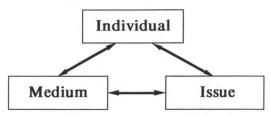

Figure 1.1   The Three-Element Model

- Finally, constructionism emphasizes the systematic integration of multiple methodologies ranging from narrowly focused experiments and content analyses to surveys and open-ended depth interviewing techniques to capture the range of meaning-constructing behavior. Rather than abandon the breadth and generalizability of traditional empirical social scientific methods for the depth, openness, and sensitivity of qualitative methods (or the other way around), a full range of methods is used in tandem (see fig. 1.2 below).

The Structure of the Book

Chapter 2 describes the research design we use as derived from the constructionist model. It is a relatively brief chapter, because many of the technical details concerning specific measurement instruments, sample sizes, and the like have been placed in a methodological appendix. The chapter is driven by a single theme, the importance of a multimethod approach to understand the process of constructing meaning. We systematically employ diverse and counterbalancing research techniques in order to triangulate and validate our findings as illustrated in figure 1.2.

We begin the study proper in Chapter 3 with an assessment of the issue environment. Drawing primarily on a series of content analyses, we review the flow of news in the United States for the period 1985 to 1987 and the relationship of our five selected issues to the broader po-

Individual

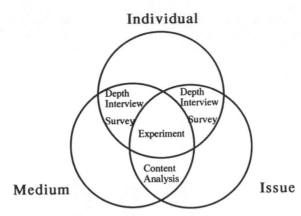

Medium   **Issue**

Figure 1.2   The Multimethod Strategy

litical context. We pay particular attention to contrasting the coverage patterns of three selected news media—television, newsmagazines, and newspapers. In that chapter we explore the presentational vocabulary, the structural syntax of news stories, and the use of visuals.

The parallel analysis of the conceptions of the five issues as held by the media and the mass public is the focus of Chapter 4. Here we contrast the journalist's imperative of objectivity with the affective style of popular discourse. We find from our transcribed depth interviews that the audience for news has little interest in the details of a particular conflict or news conference. They are concerned with the issue, broadly defined, as it impacts their own lives, their community, and nation. So we encounter a dynamic tension between the news media and their audience, as the individual viewer or reader struggles to make sense of a flurry of details, numbers, and quotations and to incorporate the significance of this new information into what they already know. News coverage tends to be dry and specific. The audience reaction, in contrast, tends to be affective and integrative. Many of the organizing issue frames of the media and individuals are similar, but they are used to different ends. We conclude that despite many parallels between the media coverage and the pictures in people's heads, there is little evidence that the media indoctrinate an inattentive or unthinking audience.

In chapters 5 and 6 we shift to our experimental and survey research instruments to look more closely at a set of thirty news stories spanning the five issues. Of our adult sample of respondents, we ask:

- What do they already know?
- What do they learn?
- How does learning vary by medium and by issue?
- How does learning vary by the cognitive skills and political interests of the individual?

Not surprisingly, what individuals might learn from a few news stories about an ongoing public issue represents a small proportion of what they already know. Although such findings are not new, they represent an important reminder of the interactive and accumulative nature of the political communication process. We turn next to evidence that directly contradicts the received wisdom about the innate inferiority of television as a news source. In this experimental context, television news proves to be more successful than newspapers in communicating substantive information to the audience. It is not, however, due to the audiovisual modality of the medium, as McLuhan and others have suggested. Indeed, the pattern is much more complex; the success of the medium as a source of political communication depends both on the nature of the public issue and the interests and backgrounds of the members of the audience.

In Chapter 6, we consider whether learning about the complex issues that confront the polity is more constrained by the ability of individuals to comprehend the material or by their interest in the topic. We find that merely paying attention to the news can compensate for the advantages of cognitive acuity. We also show that people learn some information at every level of cognitive ability, interest, and education, but that those with less acuity or prior knowledge depend significantly on the style and structure of news presentations. We show how differences in news presentation explain why television and magazine news is more accessible than newspaper news to people with average skills and interest in politics.

Chapter 7 pulls together these findings and attempts to draw out lessons for further systematic research, for democratic theory, and for journalistic practice. We conclude that the widely accepted image of an inattentive and ideologically innocent mass public drawn from three decades of survey research merits a closer look. Given the extraordinarily low likelihood that one's vote will tip an election outcome or that political authorities might actually call upon citizens to discuss their considered policy positions, political attentiveness represents a paradox. As Morris Fiorina puts it (quoted in Ferejohn, 1990, p. 13): "What is most puzzling about democratic politics is that the level of public interest is as *high* as it is, not that ignorance is widespread." Our learning experiments demonstrate that almost everybody learns at least something from a news encounter—and remembers it long enough that we can measure it. We resolve the apparent paradox of the mass public's highly figurative understanding of political issues, but only modest success in recalling news facts, in the light of Graber's admonition that "the ultimate purpose of most information gathering is the extraction of meaning" (1984, p. 151). Our study is devoted to showing how people learn and, ultimately, construct meaning about public issues, and how the print and broadcast news media can help them do it.

TWO
The Study Design

The research questions of this study center on the construction of common political knowledge in a modern industrial democracy. We ask, under what conditions are the various strata of the electorate both motivated and able to gather the information they need to play the role of active and informed citizens? And how can news and public information be made available to citizens in a way that enhances their capacity to learn about the political world around them? To answer these questions fully we would need to examine how public information is presented in the media and how it is understood by the public at large. Ideally, we would conduct an exhaustive analysis of the whole flow of news and use some nonintrusive technique to carefully monitor a large sample of individuals. We would see what these individuals attend to in news coverage, what they learn, and how they use that information to interpret and reinterpret public issues. No problem—provided we have both Gyges's ring, so that we would be invisible to the people we are studying, and the Midas touch, to provide the necessary long-term research funding.

Lacking those resources, we have settled on a strategy that attempts, nonetheless, to preserve as much as possible the strengths of an idealized study of learning through the news media, including a thorough content analysis of the media environment, systematic monitoring through surveys and experiments of what people learn from the news media they are exposed to, and depth interviews to probe how people make sense of public discourse in the media. This matched set of content analyses, surveys, laboratory experiments, and depth interviews focuses on a representative sample of issues facing the polity. It is a multimethod strategy that self-consciously attempts to play off the strengths, weaknesses, and biases of different measurement approaches to converge on a sound assessment of how the mass public learns from the media (Blalock, 1982; Brewer and Hunter, 1989).[1]

The Multimethod Design

Our choice of complementary methods rests on Hovland's important evidence that single method inquiry can seriously mislead communications research (Hovland, 1959). Hovland took up the question, Do the media have significant persuasive effects? He found that it depends on which method is used. He contrasted survey research results, which routinely demonstrated minimal media effects, with carefully controlled attitude-change experiments, which routinely produced substantial evidence of just the opposite. He concluded that a well-developed theory of communications effects would need to balance and integrate the strengths of measurement precision and validity offered by each methodological approach.

Although Hovland's sage advice was widely acknowledged at the time he wrote, it was rarely heeded. More recently, however, the idea of cross-validation through the simultaneous use of multiple methods has begun to work its way into the day-to-day practice of research. In the field of political communication, for example, Michael Robinson's widely cited study of the possible link between television news coverage and growing political malaise draws on both national survey data and extensive experimental findings (Robinson, 1976). Herbert Gans's study of American journalism creatively matches extended participant observation of journalists in action with a detailed content analysis of their output as it appears in print and on the screen (Gans, 1979). Iyengar and Kinder supplemented the painstaking series of agenda-setting experiments with a time-series analysis of changing media coverage and national public opinion data (Iyengar and Kinder, 1987).

Perhaps the most heroic example of integrated multiple methods in the communications field is Doris Graber's *Processing the News* (1988). Her study is in many ways a model for the present one. She describes her approach as following in the footsteps of Lane's extended depth interviews of fifteen New Haven men published as *Political Ideology* (1962). But her interests in the dynamic processes of attention and inattention to the flow of political information led her to expand her methodological scope to include an exhaustive content analysis of the primary news media available to her panel of twenty-one Chicago-area citizens. Also unlike Lane, she explicitly probed panelists on what they could recall and how they interpreted media coverage of the day's prominent issues.

Graber's research was conducted during an election period and her primary focus was limited to two issues, the election itself and urban crime. Because her depth interview techniques required many hours of interviewing time with each panelist, it was procedurally possible to include only twenty-one respondents. The sample size represents one of the trade-offs necessary for the depth of Graber's study of schematic cognitive processing. In this chapter we will describe the choices we have made in responding to a similar set of questions about how people conceptualize and learn about public issues in the news.

Our methodological and practical trade-offs followed a multistage strategy. First, it was necessary to select the methodologies appropriate to our hypotheses and the subject of analysis: media content, learning, and conceptualization of issues in the news. At the same time, we wanted to choose methods that would span as much as possible the dimensions of internal and external validity (Brewer and Hunter, 1989), qualitative and quantitative strengths (Nimmo and Swanson, 1990), precision and breadth (Neuman, 1989). Finally we needed to select samples of individuals, media coverage, and issues of manageable size and generalizable proportions. We will address each set of choices in turn in the following sections and then explore the actual methods used in each aspect of the study.

The Four Primary Methods: Internal and External Validity

As we noted in the previous chapter, our analysis of political communication relies on four methodological clusters: content analyses to study media coverage of issues, and depth interviews, surveys, and experiments to study individual conceptualization and mediated learning. In addition, some of our substudies (as was true in Graber's work) incorporate elements of more than one of these four methods. For example, our experiments, use a survey-like instrument to assess knowledge, attitudes and self-described behavior. In another case we asked our sample to play the role of content-analysis judges resulting in a cross between a survey and a content analysis. So, utilizing these labels a little loosely, we will proceed to explain how the data were collected and how they provide insights into news learning and issue conceptualization.

Figure 2.1 reviews the internal and external validity trade-offs among the four principal methods we employ (Cook and Campbell, 1979; Nachmias and Nachmias, 1987; Neuman, 1989). As the figure shows, our methods range from those with high external validity to those with high internal validity. In statistical analysis, internal validity indicates the strength of the causal inferences among the variables being tested. External validity refers to the generalizability of research findings to other populations or social settings, based on the representativeness of the sample and the similarity of the study situation to what might occur in the real world (Campbell and Stanley, 1963; Nachmias and Nachmias, 1987). Let us explore the validity trade-offs in the methods we have chosen for this study.

Content analyses of media coverage of the five issues provide our starting point. Our random sample of issue coverage was gathered after the fact of publication. So, although we did talk with the journalists themselves later on, we are confident that the process of our inquiry had no impact on the content of news stories. Therefore the content analyses are high on external validity; that is, they accurately reflect real-world media coverage of the issues. In contrast, however, internal validity is low. We cannot infer, from the content analysis alone, a causal connection between the media content data and what the public thinks about the issues.

Depth interviews represent an intrusion of the researcher into the lifespace of the individual. But the questions are open-ended and the setting relaxed, while the natural language of the interviewees is recorded for later analysis. The individuals being interviewed control the tone and emphasis of the discussion, so the depth interviews are relatively unintrusive and, therefore, as high as possible on external

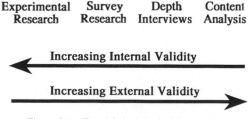

Figure 2.1   Four Methodological Approaches

validity, given the small and nonrandom sample design. We rely on the depth interviews for the most naturalistic accounts of how individuals structure their thinking and interpret the flow of media messages (Mishler, 1986; Rosenberg, 1988; Rosenberg, Ward, and Chilton, 1988; Bruner, 1990). The interviews represent our primary tool for addressing what we have termed the active construction of meaning. But the lack of structure characteristic of this kind of qualitative research means that we have only modest confidence in our ability to infer cause and effect (e.g., media influence on conceptualization) from these interviews.

Surveys, because they rely on a more structured set of questions and precoded responses, give us a somewhat more systematic and quantitative assessment of learning and thinking and move further down the scale on the trade-off between external and internal validity. The large number of respondents in the sample gives us a moderate degree of external validity as well as some internal validity from the intercorrelated responses to questions about media usage, knowledge of issues, and personal characteristics.

Finally, the most intrusive method, the classical experiment, permits greater precision in causal inference with correspondingly reduced linkage between observed and real-world behavior. In a controlled experiment, if subjects randomly assigned to different media conditions learn at different rates (unless there is an error in some aspect of the administration of the experiment), we can infer that the cause lies with the medium. But the experimental setting is not natural. Subjects are more highly motivated to pay attention during the experiment than they are at home, so the external validity is relatively weak. The series of experiments, however, explicitly brings the media, issue coverage, and subjects together in systematically varied conditions to confirm or challenge our initial conclusions drawn from the parallel analyses of media content and depth interviews.[2]

Sampling Issues, Individuals, and Media

We proceed to the last stage of our design, selecting a strategically appropriate set of public issues, media coverage of those issues, and a projectable sample of adult citizens who have come in contact with the media coverage. The aim of the sampling was to allow meaningful comparisons among issues, media, and individuals.

Issues in the News

The daily flow of news and public information to the modern American citizen is overwhelming. An earlier study found that the average adult is exposed daily to over 60,000 "words" of information from the various mass media (Neuman and Pool, 1986, p. 74). A television set throws forth 3,600 images a minute. The average daily newspaper contains over 150,000 words and several thousand images. The challenge of sampling the flow of news information over a three-year period is daunting. Even though most citizens are simply forced to ignore the great majority of news stories available to them, we estimate that the average citizen will have read or viewed well over 15,000 news stories during the three-year period of our study.

Although at the level of words and images the task seems nearly impossible, at the level of fundamental public issues facing the country, the task of sampling issues rather than bits of information is not nearly so hard. Indeed, the majority of those 15,000 stories are ephemeral tidbits concerning the day's weather, traffic, stock market movements, sports scores, and the like, not the material of sustained political contemplation. And of the other stories, most weave together naturally as a fabric of continuing themes, concerning issues of national and local economic well-being, social inequality, race relations, the environment, international relations, and public health and such.

At the outset of the study, we elaborated a list of ongoing and recurring public issues that seemed to dominate the news and public concern. We set aside political election coverage as a special case. We did not want to settle on a particularly unusual or especially dramatic story, such as the Challenger space shuttle disaster in January 1986, or one that seemed to slip by public attention despite extensive coverage, such as the controversial nomination of Robert Bork to the Supreme Court in 1987. We sought stories and public reactions in the middle ground, with moderate levels of media coverage and public response, topics most citizens would recognize and about which they would know something, but not major media events. We considered a range of issues, including abortion, tax reform, the Middle East, and the environment, but found that some topics posed difficulties in locating parallel stories across media for use in the experimental portion of the study.

Finally we settled on five issues: apartheid in South Africa, Star

Wars, the stock market crash of October 1987, drug abuse, and AIDS. These issues exemplify many of the themes of public concern for this period, as we will demonstrate in the following chapter. The Strategic Defense Initiative (SDI), was selected to reflect both nuclear proliferation and technology issues. The stock market crash of October 1987 marked a sharp downturn in the economy that some economists attributed at least in part to the growing federal deficit. Drug abuse and AIDS are serious social and health problems that call for mass education campaigns and the allocation of resources. Finally, apartheid in South Africa was selected in order to include an issue of international scope and domestic resonance in the analysis.

Of course, no set of five issues could possibly cover the full breadth and complexity of the flow of news for this period, but these stories do draw on a number of broad questions confronting the nation in the last decades of the twentieth century. South Africa and SDI represent the kind of issues with which only a very few citizens have any direct contact or expertise, but are widely recognized and are mentioned repeatedly in connection with events, public speeches, and protests. Drug abuse and AIDS are issues on a more human scale with which many individuals have personal experience independent of media coverage. They are, nonetheless, public issues, and the news stories with which we worked repeatedly discussed questions of appropriate public policy to handle these problems. Because both drugs and AIDS deal in part with socially marginal groups, they often draw out deeply held social values as citizens react to and interpret the news. The stock market crash was an event that influenced the economic life of all Americans but, because of the technical character of the subject and the ambiguity of its effects, remained obscure to many citizens.

These issues span the gamut from economics to national security, public health, race relations, technology, and the proper role of government. Each is tied to an event or series of ongoing events that bring the "issue" repeatedly to the attention of the news audience for further consideration. Each has complex technical and institutional elements and historical precedents. Together they represent a rich starting point for the study of media coverage and the public response.

Further details on the news environment and the public's collective sense of what is and is not important will be addressed at the outset of Chapter 3, and information on the story sample and the validity of its representativeness is provided in the Methodological Appendix.

Sampling the Mass Public

Our experiments and depth interviews were conducted at the MIT Media Laboratory's Audience Research Facility at the Liberty Tree Mall, in Danvers, Massachusetts. Subjects were recruited from the population of 25,000 daily shoppers by employing a "mall intercept" quota sampling technique (Rothenberg, 1989; Linz et al., 1991). Eight separate experiments were conducted averaging over 180 subjects per experiment for a total of about 1,300 subjects. A subsample of 43 respondents were re-interviewed in extended and loosely structured depth interviews which lasted from one to two hours (see Appendix table A.1).

Subject recruitment was carefully stratified by a variety of demographic variables to match as closely as possible the population distribution of Essex County, in which the research facility is located. In order to assure a broad range of subjects, recruiters informed prospects only that they would participate in media research, and the news focus of the inquiry was not revealed until the experiment was under way. To assure comparable experimental groups, strict random assignment was used to select each subject's exposure condition.

Sampling Media

Our research focuses on a comparison of three primary national news media—network television news, newsmagazines, and newspapers. In the case of newspapers, we avoided the traditional research emphasis on the newspapers of record, such as the *New York Times* or *Washington Post*, and chose instead to use the *Boston Globe*, the dominant newspaper of the metropolitan region in which the research was conducted. Given that our sampling of stories was highly constrained by the need to find naturally occurring, parallel content in three different news media, a complex sampling frame of newspapers or wire service coverage was neither practical nor appropriate. Of course we cannot assert that the *Globe*'s coverage of the issues and usage of wire stories is or is not representative of what the average American newspaper reader is likely to read, because newspaper styles and substance vary enormously across the country. Assessments of the hierarchy of American newspapers tend to put the *Globe* in the top tier, but below the prestige press.

We had initially tried also to incorporate radio news in the study but found that in network radio news, issue coverage is so brief and fleeting that radio source materials were not at all comparable to the other media under study. In the world of radio, National Public Radio's "All Things Considered" is a notable exception to the rule. It would have made a most interesting news source for systematic study. In the end, we decided not to incorporate the program because of the fact that it is, indeed, one of a kind and more representative of what radio could be rather than what radio tends to be. Radio talk shows, because they incorporate both the presentation of public information from "experts" as well as public reaction, would also have made an interesting source. But again because of their special, nonexpository character, we set them aside for another inquiry. We turn now to a description of the methods used in each aspect of the analysis—media content, individual conceptualization, and learning from the news media.

The Content Analyses

To maintain a real-world perspective on the news, we placed our analysis of the five issues into the context of the news of the period. Utilizing published indices, we assessed the coverage of prominent political and social issues in a broad sample of newspapers, newsmagazines, and network newscasts for the period 1985–87. From this overview of the total news environment, we gained perspective on the relative media prominence of the issues we chose to study. We then made a detailed analysis of a sample of 150 news stories from the five issue areas that arc thc focus of our experiments and in-depth interviews. The news sample was drawn from the same sources from which we selected the stimulus materials used in the experiments—that is, news stories in the *Boston Globe*, newsmagazines (*Time, Newsweek, US News and World Report*), and network newscasts for the period 1985–87 (see Appendix table A.2). Quantitative assessments were made by analyzing several presentational characteristics of news—for example, the use of human interest narratives, abstract political concepts, background information, and visual images—as well as the structural syntax of news stories. We applied the same kind of assessments made on the three-year media sample to the television, newspaper, and newsmagazine stories actually used in the experiments (see Appendix table A.3).

The content analyses were designed to validate and confirm that the content materials we used in the experiments were indeed representative of the broader flow and trends in media coverage for the period and to assess which factors in the content and story structure in each of the media were related to the avoidance of or learning of political information.

The Individual Depth Interviews

The purpose of the depth interviews was to try to probe for a deeper understanding of how a subset of our subjects conceptualize public policy issues and interpret the information they see and hear in the news media. The focus of the depth interview was not so much to understand how or what people learn from different media, but rather to put our analyses in the context of the individual's natural framing of the issues (Goffman, 1974; Gamson, 1989; Crigler and Jensen, 1991). The depth interviews also helped to uncover the strategies people use for filtering and managing the information flow in the broadcast and print media they habitually use.

The depth interviews were tape recorded and transcribed, loosely structured discussions based on six "starter" questions and lasting approximately one to two hours per person (see Appendix). Trained interviewers were instructed to let the interviewee do most of the talking and speak freely about whatever subjects came to his or her mind. The intention of this method places emphasis on the individual's structuring of issues and opinions, rather than on the individual's fitting of views to an interviewer's questions, expectations, or possible response categories. The interviews were to elicit information from people "in their own voices" rather than to rely solely on the strict replicability of a structured interview (Mishler, 1986).

The transcription and analysis of natural-language-based conversations has the distinct advantage of sensitizing the researchers to the differences between their own and their interviewees' manner of conceptualizing politics (Mishler, 1986; Polanyi, 1989; Bruner, 1990). As the richness of this method lies in the person's own words, the interviews were listened to and read for frames that emerged from the discourse, rather than coded into predetermined categories. Intercoder reliability was ensured by having multiple reading teams. The teams read each interview aloud, discussing and noting the frames that were used in the discourse; then they listened to the tapes for validation of the transcripts and the frames. This procedure was repeated for each interview, after which the teams met to compare results. The individual's use of frames to conceptualize the same issues and the journalist's framing of issues in news stories were compared for similarities and differences.

The Surveys

The surveys were designed to complement the findings of the necessarily small depth interview sample as well as to provide background information about the experimental subjects. We employed both primary and secondary survey analyses in this project. Table 2.1 provides an overview of the surveys we used. Those studies listed as "primary analyses" were conducted with intercept quota samples at the Audience Research Facility in Danvers, Massachusetts, as part of the experimental study series or piggy-backed onto other projects which were undertaken at the facility. The "secondary analyses" refer to national telephone and in-home-interview data sets collected by other researchers and from which we have drawn supplemental and comparative findings for our analysis.

Table 2.1   Survey Studies

Primary Analyses (No. of Cases)

	South Africa	SDI	Crash	Drugs	AIDS	Total
Issue knowledge	368	333	175	305	182	1,363

	Television News	Newsmagazine	Newspaper	Total
Media attributes and behavior	1,363	1,363	1,363	1,363
Media evaluations	155	155	166	166

Secondary Analyses

Gallup Poll: American Institute of Public Opinion Research
Times Mirror News Interest Index: Times Mirror Center for the People and the Press

The data on issue knowledge and media attributes and behavior were collected as part of pretest materials in the experimental study series. We asked both closed and open-ended questions about news media use and preferences, issue knowledge, and, for all five issues, relative rankings of overall importance. The total sample size is 1,363. Because of the number of items involved, however, separate issue information indices are based on subsamples of from 175 to 368 respondents.

The media evaluations survey was conducted separately. Respondents were asked to evaluate various generic news media (television, magazines, and newspapers) and specific media and programs (CBS Evening News with Dan Rather, *Time* magazine, and the *Boston Globe*) concerning their relative strengths in providing entertainment and information. The sample size for this study numbered 166.

For additional information and to validate the survey findings based on our local intercept surveys, we turned as well to several archived national studies. The Gallup organization, for example, has for many years asked its respondents at regular intervals to identify the "most important problems" facing the country at the time of the survey. We drew on that data for the 1985–87 period to help evaluate the nature of the public perception of the news environment during our study period. The *Times Mirror News Index* provides similar national level data using a different methodology. The survey results are used at various points in each of chapters 3–6.

The Media and Modality Experiments

The question we wanted the experiments to answer was, How much difference does the style of journalism and modality of communication make in what people learn from the news? In order to isolate the effects of style and mode, we conducted two kinds of experiments as illustrated in table 2.2.

In the cross-media series of experiments, we compared what subjects learned from naturally occurring news stories on TV, in newsmagazines, and in newspapers. News items were selected so that the same substantive information was included in each medium's version of the story, but the journalistic presentation varied as it actually does by medium (see Appendix for news story samples). Any differences in what subjects learned reflect the natural differences among the media

Table 2.2   The Media and Modality Experiments (No. of Cases)

	South Africa	SDI	Crash	Drugs	AIDS	Total
Media experiments						
Network TV news	61	66	55	56	60	298
Newsmagazine	65	64	59	59	62	309
Newspaper	61	66	61	60	60	308
Total	187	196	175	175	182	915
Modality experiments I						
Video	60	45	—	45	—	150
Audio	61	47	—	40	—	148
Print	60	45	—	40	—	145
Total	181	137	—	125	—	443
Audience evaluation study						
Network TV news	20	20	20	20	20	100
Newsmagazine	20	20	20	20	20	100
Newspaper	20	20	20	20	20	100
Total	60	60	60	60	60	300

and could be due either to the modality of communication (e.g., TV or print) or differences in presentation that characterize a television news story, a newsmagazine story, or a newspaper story.

In order to separate these causal links, we conducted several additional experiments that focused exclusively on differences in communication modality. In these experiments, television coverage of the news stories was decomposed into an audio-only condition and also transcribed and typeset to simulate print media. The verbal text of the news stories was the same in each condition and variation was limited to the mode of communication (audio, print, and audiovisual). Because the textual/auditory content was the same in each condition, any differences in learning by subjects in different modality conditions can, therefore, be attributed exclusively to the mode of communication. In both sets of experiments, internal validity was assessed with a number of additional controls in single experiments, including post-only and stimulus-post-only conditions. We also draw on a related study which includes a visual-only condition. Of course any experiment introduces an element of artificiality into the context of the behavior. A particular problem in learning experiments is that the subjects are "on task" and cued to performance in a way they would not be in the natural setting. Our experiments were designed to reduce "cuing" by introducing a series of distractor tasks prior to exposure to the news stories (see Appendix tables A.6–A.8).

Our experimental design, in contrast with survey research, makes it possible for us to distinguish pre-existing political knowledge from actual media learning. The principal tool for measuring political learning was a twelve- to sixteen-item "true/false/don't know" checklist, which was administered in both the pre- and post-test to assess information gain (see Appendix table A.7). This Information Index includes items referring to facts as well as common misunderstandings related to each of the news stories. All the information required for correctly answering each item was common to each of the three media versions of the news stories in the cross-media experiments. Our aim in using a true/false/don't know format was not to put an undue burden on the subjects' short-term memories by providing ample cues.

We have also taken particular pains to include independent measures of cognitive ability in our experiments and not to rely on convenient but potentially misleading socioeconomic characteristics as surrogate measures for intellectual capacity. Our design, utilizing a broad-based sample and including a specific cognitive skills measure in the questionnaire, makes possible an explicit test of the role of cognitive ability in political learning from the mass media (see Appendix table A.6).

Finally, we also conducted a study that is, in effect, a cross between an experiment and a content analysis—the Audience Evaluation Study. To move beyond the traditional approach of content analysis based on objective expert measurements, we decided as well to enlist a panel of nonexpert judges to test whether the traditional academic distinctions and categories make much sense to the mass audience and to solicit a broad based, subjective response to news style and content. We drew the nonexpert judges from the same population as our experimental subjects. Judges were asked to rate the stimulus stories on analytic continua which previous research had suggested might be related to learning from the news media (Gunter, 1987; Robinson and Levy, 1987; Graber, 1988). (See Appendix table A.4). Each panel judged four stimulus stories (two stories for each issue) in one of the experimental conditions.

Interviews with Journalists

As a supplemental methodology, we directed a graduate research project that involved extended telephone interviews in the spring of

1988 with eighteen of the journalists who wrote the thirty stories selected for use in the experiments (Kiolbassa, 1989). The discussions ranged from twenty-five to forty-five minutes in length and focused on what the journalists intended the stories to convey, how well they thought the medium was suited to the story, why and how they constructed the story the way they did, and what impact they thought the story had on the audience.

The interviews involved journalists from CBS News, *Time* magazine, and the *Boston Globe* and included Art Buchwald (who is syndicated in the *Globe*), Bernard Goldberg and Terry Drinkwater from CBS News, and Richard Stengel at *Time*. The journalists were sent copies or transcripts of the stories they had written; they were then interviewed by phone to discuss the individual stories and the broader public issues related to the stories, as well as the general news environment. Unlike sociological field studies, the project did not involve extensive participant observation (Breed, 1955; Cohen, 1963; Epstein, 1973; Sigal, 1973; Altheide, 1976; Tuchman, 1978; Gans, 1979). Our focus here is on the interaction of media, issues, and audience, but we did want to take a closer look at how the process looks from the media side.

An Overview

We begin our study by reviewing the issue environment of the late 1980s, utilizing the range of content analysis techniques described here and in the Appendix. In the following chapters we compare the results of our content analysis of the media with data about the mass audience drawn from depth interviews, surveys, and experiments. Chapter 4 focuses on public conceptualization of issues as revealed in the depth interviews and contrasts those with media presentations. Chapters 5 and 6 draw on the experimental results to explore what people learn from the media about the issues, whether there are systematic differences in learning from television, magazines, and newspapers, and how different audience strata interact with news media presentations. In Chapter 5 we also draw briefly on depth interviews with journalists actively involved in these five issue areas to contrast what we have learned from our research with the accumulated field wisdom of practicing news professionals.

In selecting these techniques, we have brought together the advantages of a variety of research approaches to political learning: (1) the diversity and larger sample sizes of mass sample surveys, (2) the less intrusive and less artificial quality of natural-language depth interviews, (3) the precision of measurement and strength of causal inference from experiments which utilized representative real-world stimuli and adult subjects, (4) the breadth and representativeness of systematically sampled, large-scale content analyses, and (5) extended telephone interviews to gain the otherwise missing perspective of the journalists themselves who are caught up in the complex structural constraints of institutionalized commercial journalism. Each method has its limits. But by comparison with each other and the accumulated research literature of the field, we attempt to piece together a realistic and robust assessment of political learning from the news media and the construction of common knowledge.

THREE
Five Issues, Three News Media

Even the most casual assessment of the daily flow of news reveals a complex tapestry of issues and events, some of which appear and reappear over a long period of time, and others which flash briefly in the headlines and then disappear. The more we look at the news, the more we are impressed with the difficulty of building enduring conceptualizations for the fragments of ideas, events, opinions, facts, and images that constitute the news on any given day.

In the last chapter we reviewed the problem of deriving a representative sample of news stories from the approximately 5,000 or so items that the average individual will view, hear, or read in the mass media during a typical year. The key to making what would otherwise be an unmanageable task manageable (both for the news audience and the research analyst) is the concept of *issues* in the news—broadly defined and enduring problems, public concerns, or points of controversy on which both journalists and citizens rely heavily for making sense of the news and "taming the information tide."

The relationship between a news story and a news issue is central to our analysis. When we refer to making sense of the news or constructing political meaning, the corresponding microlevel process for the individual is, in effect, linking a news story (by definition, new information) to a news issue and an interpretive frame (what they already know). Different individuals, of course, can interpret the same story in dramatically different ways. This is the concept of interpretive polysemy emphasized in the traditions of reception analysis and cultural studies, a topic we turn to in the next chapter (Barkin and Gurevitch, 1987; Livingstone, 1989; Jensen and Rosengren, 1990; Jensen, 1990). How issues evolve in public thought over time has become an increasingly important area of public opinion research (Downs, 1972; Miller and Levitin, 1976; Carmines and Stimson, 1989). Our purpose in this chapter is to review the news environment of the mid 1980s in the United States and take a closer look at the five issues that serve as the focal point of our analysis. Following our interest in the "television hypothesis," a recurring theme in our study will be comparative content analyses across media and an analysis of the public response to these patterns.

Late Reagan

Our study covers the period 1985 through 1988. It was a relatively quiet period in American social, political, and economic life, in many ways parallel to what has been characterized as the quiescent fifties, the Eisenhower years (Miller and Levitin, 1976; Nie, Verba, and Petrocik, 1976). After a twenty-year slide of growing dissatisfaction with the quality of government, there were signs of a distinct rebounding of confidence and trust (Lipset, 1985; Citrin, Green, and Reingold, 1987). Reagan's approval ratings after a brief dip in late 1982 crept back up to unprecedentedly high levels until the Iran-Contra affair took a relatively modest toll on Reagan's popularity in 1987. The economy also rebounded with robust health and vigor from the recession of 1981–82 and, until the stock market crash of October 1987, showed few apparent signs of weakness. A number of professional economists as well as some business leaders and some politicians became increasingly alarmed with the growing deficit as a difficult legacy of supply-side economic policies, but their concerns were generally not mirrored by the general public (Modigliani and Modigliani, 1987; Ladd, 1988).

The mid-1980s were also characterized by relative quiet on the international front. The emotion and controversy associated with Vietnam and the Iranian crisis had receded, but a cold war mentality was still dominant. The evolution of *glasnost* and Soviet economic reform were still at very early stages, and the opening of Eastern Europe had not yet occurred. Violence in Afghanistan, Northern Ireland, and South Africa was geographically distant and did not directly involve American lives. There were scattered acts of terrorism in the Middle East and the intensification of the *intifada* on the West Bank, but nothing approaching the scale of the Gulf War to come four years later. Reagan's approval ratings for dealing with the Soviet Union held steady at 60+ percent, and his approval rating for overall international affairs did not drop until 1987, again as a result of the Iran-Contra affair, and it rebounded to the original positive levels by 1988 (*Opinion Roundup*, 1988b).

The late Reagan era was not bereft of social problems and political tensions, but there were no energy or hostage crises, no Watergate or Gulf War. It was a period between elections. Our emphasis, therefore, is not on media and public opinion during national crises or at the pinnacle of the four-year election cycle. This is a study of day-to-day news and politics as usual.

The Public Agenda and the Media Agenda

Research on public and media issue agendas generally identify nine broad categories of public life or a subset of the nine with occasionally expanded subcategories, depending on the purpose of the research.[1] The categories—politics, economics, international relations/defense, the environment, health, poverty, race relations, crime, and morality—are surprisingly durable over many decades. The Gallup Poll's "most important problem" topics for this period are summarized according to this scheme in table 3.1.

When we review the biggest news stories, we see a somewhat different picture of the overall news environment for this period. The data in table 3.2 are derived from the Conference on Issues and Media's "National Media Index," a running content analysis of newspaper, newsmagazine, and network television news coverage patterns, and the *Times Mirror* monthly national survey of news interest which reports the percentage of the adult population "very closely following" specific news stories.

Individual news stories, we see, are event- and people-centered and are tied to broader issues in complex ways. Late-breaking stories of life and death drama capture the top of the list. Little Jessica McClure falling into an abandoned well in Texas is notable, because what would otherwise have been a personal and private tragedy evolved into a media event with, fortunately, a happy ending. Surely, most citizens would identify the state of the economy, crime, and AIDS as more "important" and enduring issues than Jessica McClure. But what attracts their attention in the news, they freely admit, is a mixture of what is important and what is immediately and personally relevant and humanly dramatic.

Table 3.1   Public Opinion Data on Most Important Problem, 1985–87 (%)

	1985	1986	1987
Politics			
Dissatisfied with gov't	—	—	03
Economics			
Unemployment	17	16	12
Deficit	14	11	09
Cost of living	06	05	02
Economy (general)	05	04	08
International relations			
Threat of war	00	07	07
Nuclear arms race	05	03	05
Environment	—	—	—
Health			
AIDS	—	—	02
Poverty			
Poverty/Hunger	05	06	04
Race	—	—	—
Crime			
Crime	03	02	03
Drug abuse	02	02	08
Morality			
Moral decline	02	03	04

Source: Gallup Poll.

Table 3.2 reveals a complex tension between, on the one hand, stories of concrete human drama and immediate relevance and, on the other, difficult, complex, distant but "important" enduring issues and social problems. This tension will guide our analysis of what an issue is and how both journalists and typical citizens struggle to make sense of the "world outside."

Another implication of table 3.2 is that we are seeing evidence of a very active and independent-minded audience. The correlation between amount of media coverage and public response is hardly dramatic evidence of agenda-setting. Sometimes the media and the public see eye to eye on what is worth following closely (Challenger); sometimes not (Chernobyl). This finding is consonant with developments in communications theory. The new work in the agenda-setting tradition is moving away from simple correlations to developing a theory of

Table 3.2   Major News Stories, 1986–87

Peak Percentage of National Media Coverage[a]	Percentage of Public Who Follow Story Very Closely[b]	News Story
31	80	Space Shuttle Challenger Disaster, 1986
—	69	Little Girl Falls in Well in Texas, 1987
28	33	Iran-Contra Affair, 1986–87
28	40	Stock Market Crash October, 1987
28	19	U.S. Soviet Relations
25	—	Philippines Elections
24	58	U.S. Air Strikes against Libya, 1986
21	38	Persian Gulf "Tanker War," 1986
18	46	Chernobyl Disaster, 1986
17	—	Pope John Paul II Trip to U.S., 1987
14	15	Presidential Campaign, 1987
13	—	South Africa, 1986
12	28	Gary Hart Scandal, 1987
11	48	TWA Hostage Crisis, 1986

[a] *National Media Index.*
[b] *Times Mirror News Interest Index.*

what kinds of public issues and under what political conditions media effects are most evident (McCombs, 1981).

Five Issues in the News

Issues endure for decades; news stories are by their nature ephemeral. Anthony Downs has developed an intriguing theory of the life cycle of a social problem as a newsworthy issue (Downs, 1972). He posits that a triggering event catapults a problem to public attention. There is a period of generalized public concern and usually a number of government initiatives in the area. But inevitably attention wanes, the issue loses its ability to capture public attention, and its place is taken by new issues. Finally, he notes ironically that little is likely to have changed in the fundamentals of the problem itself at any point in the attention cycle. But, as Lippmann frequently asserts, no doubt it is better that the issue rose to public attention, if only briefly, than not at all.

This study, as we noted in the previous chapter, is not designed to assess the dynamics of issue evolution and decline over time. It is instead a snapshot approach. We capture media coverage and public thinking on five issues in midstream. But the snapshot is a close-up, and it allows us to examine the patterns of learning and interpretation in some detail.

We cannot incorporate a very large portion of the issue agenda of the mid-1980s in our content analyses, learning experiments, and depth interviews. The selection of five issues represents both the strength and weakness of our approach. However, even with only five issues, the coverage is surprisingly complete. Of the nine issue categories in general research use, for example, we capture significant parts of seven.

The stock market crash and the assessment of its causes and consequences draw out virtually all of the prominent economic issues raised as "most important problems," including the deficit, employment patterns, and the health of the economy. The SDI stories involve the key issues of war and peace, superpower relations, and high technology. The AIDS stories concern issues of public health, federal health policy, and because of the connection to sexual behavior and drug use, many related issues of public morality and alternative life-styles. The apartheid stories involve issues of race and of international relations in the Third World. The drug stories draw in issues of public health, poverty, race, and, of course, crime. The five sets of stories, however, do not deal directly with political institutions and electoral politics, or with environmental issues.

South Africa

News from or about South Africa was virtually never out of the public eye in the United States during the period 1985–87. South African news averaged just under 3 percent of the total national and international news volume, peaking at 8.3 percent in the summer and fall of 1985.[2] This was a time of South Africa's press boycott, which proved to be counterproductive (from the point of view of South African authorities) as it taunted foreign journalists into covering the racial violence with renewed energy and added the theme of press restriction and repression as a new and dramatic element to each story.

It is interesting to note that the South African government itself appears to subscribe to the "television hypothesis." It went to great lengths to ban television cameras but not necessarily reporters from the scenes of racial violence. The government characterized video coverage of violence as a primary incitement to further violence and deemed that the visuals distracted attention from the message the authorities wished to put forward.

Nelson Mandela was still in jail. The restrictions of apartheid were not changed, nor were any new proposals for change evident within the Botha regime. Continuing violence in South Africa and a steady stream of protests in the United States and Europe in favor of financial divestment continued to draw world attention.

We selected two news stories from this period for our experimental analysis. The first dealt with the execution of a black poet and supporter of the outlawed African National Congress named Benjamin Moloise despite international and internal pleas for clemency. He had been convicted of murdering a black policeman two years earlier. After the execution, black supporters of Moloise poured onto the streets of Cape Town and Johannesburg and battled police in a violent four-hour confrontation. American media coverage included graphic images of the violence and explained the background of the Moloise case. The second story dealt with the attempted press ban itself and the failure of the ban to lower the level of racial violence within South Africa.

The Strategic Defense Initiative

The Strategic Defense Initiative was a focal point of Reagan's defense policy and Soviet negotiating strategy through the mid-1980s. Proposed in a dramatic speech in 1983, SDI, Reagan claimed, would render nuclear weapons obsolete, a claim frequently echoed in the media (Manoff, 1989). The controversy over SDI concerned its cost and technical feasibility. Some have argued, however, that the underlying question of whether SDI would really work did not matter as long as Gorbachev and his advisors believed that it would. Federal expenditures on strategic missile defenses grew from one to four billion dollars annually during the interval between 1982 and 1987, accompanied by much fanfare and debate, although the expenditures were still less than half of the equivalent annual investment in strategic missile defenses at the height of the Cold War in the 1950s and early 1960s (Lakoff and

York, 1989, p. 50). News coverage of SDI peaked at regular intervals associated with budget negotiations, summit meetings, or domestic debates over the program's scientific and strategic soundness. SDI news averaged .5 percent of total news volume for 1985–87, reaching a maximum of 1 percent in the late fall of 1985. The public was split on whether SDI was a good idea and worth the investment, with those in favor outnumbering those opposed by 50 percent to 40 percent, on average, with a surprisingly low 10 percent undecided (Bard 1987).

The first story on SDI used in the experimental studies dealt with the technology itself, how it was supposed to work and the scientific controversy over its feasibility. Photographs and illustrations of satellites, lasers, and "smart rocks" systems illustrated the debate. The second story focused on the public relations wars between pro-SDI lobbyists and the more skeptical Union of Concerned Scientists, both of which developed television spots focusing on a child's understanding of how a space shield would work. Both spots were extensively covered in news reports of the print and broadcast media. The stories emphasized the central issue of whether SDI might lead to a false sense of security and carelessness in the difficult matters of superpower relations.

The Stock Market Crash of 1987

On Black Monday, October 19, 1987, the Dow Jones Index dropped 508 points, a loss of over 22 percent of the market's value in a single day, part of the "paper loss" that week that approached a trillion dollars. Investor confidence was shaken. The economy was in a tailspin. Virtually every commentator noted that the depth and suddenness of the decline exceeded early stages of the crash of 1929. We know now that the two events are not at all parallel. But at the time the reporters were reporting and our subjects were attempting to interpret the profusion of figures and media analysis, what it meant was not at all clear.

The media reports, however, emphasized two points: (1) that there were numerous experts who blamed the fall directly on Reagan's economic policies, and (2) that the effects of the market decline would not be limited to well-to-do investors but would be felt by every element of the American economy. In non-crisis times, stock market news averages just over 1 percent of the news flow, but much of that reportage is quite routine and uninteresting to noninvestors. Market-related news jumped to over 7 percent of the news flow for the fourth quarter of 1987, peaking at 28 percent immediately following the crash. We picked two crash-related stories for our experimental analyses, one focusing on the causes of the crash and one focusing on its effects. Few words were minced in either domain. *Time* began its piece on the causes of the crash with two quotations, the first from economist Otto Eckstein: "Reagan's economic policy is an off-the-wall approach. We're running an incredible experiment with these budget and trade deficits"; the second from Chrysler's Lee Iacocca: "It is a scandal. I don't know what they're on down in Washington. It's wacko time."

The television versions were equally pointed, although a bit more visually oriented. ABC's Economic Editor Dan Corditz, for example, with appropriate graphic support, began his report: "Remember the old cartoon where Wiley Coyote runs off a cliff and it takes him a while to recognize that there is nothing holding him up? Something very much like that happened to the stock market."

Cocaine and Drug Abuse

Cocaine and crack are sold and consumed in very small amounts, most often measured in fractions of an ounce. So if the U.S. Drug Enforcement Agency's 1985 estimate of U.S. cocaine consumption is even close, cocaine is a big problem. They estimated 100 tons. The following year a University of Michigan medical researcher labeled cocaine the nation's most serious drug problem. By 1988 the National Institute of Drug Abuse released research on usage: 20 million Americans had experimented with cocaine and crack, and 5 million were active and regular users. The linkage to crime was made clear. NIDA estimates $60 billion in losses directly attributable to cocaine-linked criminal behavior.

Drug stories were in the national news throughout this period with an average 1.7 percent of the news flow, and peaking at 4.7 percent in mid-1986 just after college basketball star Len Bias's sudden death was revealed to be a cocaine overdose. Just as the revelation that Rock Hudson had died of AIDS made the disease a public issue, the Len Bias case in June 1986 initiated a flow of stories identifying crack as more dangerous and detrimental than heroine. The emphasis of most stories at this point was on the drug abusers and their families as victims and on the victims of drug related crimes. Of the stories in our experimental sample, one focused on the crack-crime connection in urban ghettos, and the second focused on the effects on infant children of a mother's cocaine addiction during pregnancy. Later in 1988 and 1989, the emphasis in news coverage would shift again to issues of drug trafficking and drug enforcement.

The AIDS Crisis

By 1988, virtually 100 percent of the American population had heard about AIDS and had some idea of its origins and its effects on its victims (*Opinion Roundup*, 1988a). In early 1985, AIDS made up 10 percent of health-related news stories; by the fall, after the death of Rock Hudson, it dominated 55 percent of the health news coverage. Overall AIDS stories represented 1.6 percent of the national news volume, peaking at 3.3 percent in mid-1987. The public was well aware that homosexual contact with an infected partner or sharing needles with infected drug users were the primary risks, yet 42 percent in a 1988 Gallup survey admitted that they were at least somewhat concerned that they would contract the disease themselves (*Opinion Roundup*, 1988a).

The U.S. Centers for Disease Control in Atlanta estimated that by 1988 one million Americans were infected with the AIDS virus. Because AIDS may remain dormant for many years, the number of documented cases is lower: 48,000 confirmed cases and 27,000 confirmed deaths attributable to AIDS.

One of our experimental stories dealt with a 1986 National Academy of Sciences report on the state of the AIDS epidemic and its impact on the nation's health and health care system. The other dealt with a proposal for mandatory AIDS testing and the impact of the crisis on the gay community and public attitudes toward homosexuality.

Television, Newsmagazines, and Newspapers

In the evolution of the modern mass media, each major medium in turn has served as the dominant negative symbol of mass culture. First the penny newspaper in the 1830s, the general interest mass magazine in the 1890s, radio in the 1920s, motion pictures in the 1930s, and television from the 1950s onward. As both Lowery and De Fleur (1983) and Wartella and Reeves (1985) ably demonstrate, each new messenger becomes a target of blame for much of what ails mass society. Radio was a tool of authoritarian propagandists and contributed to the rise of Naziism. Motion pictures caused juvenile delinquency (as did the evolution of dime novels in the decades before and comic books in the decade which followed.) Now television takes the blame for everything from decreasing national Scholastic Aptitude Test scores to the decline of political parties and the possible demise of democracy itself (Manheim, 1976; Mander, 1978).

In this context we use the phrase the "television hypothesis" as a convenient shorthand to identify what is, in effect, a more complex set of propositions about differences among a variety of news media, their psychophysical characteristics, their independent journalistic traditions, and their varying audience attitudes and presumptions.

The Television Hypothesis

As we noted in the first chapter, extensive research has been conducted on the differences in the way newspapers, magazines, and television cover public issues. Analysis focused on the structural constraints that result in different journalistic styles (Robinson, 1972; Epstein, 1973; Weaver, 1975; Gans, 1979; Robinson and Sheehan, 1983; Robinson and Levy, 1986; Graber, 1987; Iyengar and Kinder, 1987; Bennett, 1988). Studies that compare media presentation generally find that television news is much more entertaining and involving than print media (Robinson and Levy, 1986), while newspapers are credited with providing more information and more context for information.

Observers have noted that television stories are designed to have exciting visuals and a narrative structure (a beginning, middle, and end) and to personalize the story in order to hold the audience's attention throughout the news program. Most analysts view the entertainment and narrative elements of television news in a negative light, arguing that their combined effects trivialize issues and distract from understanding (Epstein, 1973; Robinson and Sheehan, 1983; Bennett, 1988).

By way of contrast, newspapers are praised for providing in-depth coverage of news. Numerous studies argue that newspapers provide a breadth and organization of information which is a positive contribution to learning, not as readily available on television (Fang, 1972; Manoff and Schudson, 1986; Abel, 1981). Analysts point to the newspaper's inverted pyramid structure, which organizes the facts of a story in order of importance. Moreover, print media permit the audience to select which items to attend to and to refer back and review a passage for more complete understanding.

While newsmagazines share with newspapers the modality of print, the weekly news magazines have a different structural bias—an emphasis on the historical, economic, and political contexts of the week's events. Newsmagazines combine some of the breadth of subject matter found in newspapers with some of the entertainment factors (e.g., attractive visual presentation and lively news writing) of television (Henry, 1985).

We decided to see how these generally accepted findings about the way media cover public affairs apply to the presentation of the five issues we had chosen to study. Our concern here is not only on whether the media provided coverage but on how effectively they made information available to the public. To answer these questions we employed three strategies: an objective coding of various manifest elements of the news stories, an audience response evaluation to get at the more affective and latent aspects of news presentation, and a series of news experiments to which we will turn in chapters 5 and 6.

Table 3.3 responds to the question of differential news agendas by tabulating the coverage of our five issues on television, in magazines, and newspapers. We collected the data for each issue under index

Table 3.3   Media Coverage of the Five Issues

	TV			Magazine			Newspaper		
	%	No. of Stories	No. of Words*	%	No. of Stories	No. of Words*	%	No. of Stories	No. of Words*
S. Africa	46	911	328	7	19	10	31	1,644	1,503
SDI	8	153	55	9	25	30	10	509	326
Crash	6	124	45	27	75	88	20	1,046	670
Drugs	20	410	147	30	84	99	20	1,124	720
AIDS	20	403	145	27	74	88	18	922	591

*In thousands of words.

Note: Figures are the average number of index listings per network or publication for each issue from 1985 to 1987 included in the *Vanderbilt Television News Archive*, *Boston Globe Index*, and the listings for the three largest newsmagazines included in the *Readers' Guide to Periodical Literature*.

headings in the *Vanderbilt Television News Archive,* the *Boston Globe Index,* and newsmagazines in the *Reader's Guide to Periodical Literature.* Table 3.3 provides no evidence that television news coverage is idiosyncratic. Patterns of coverage vary among the media somewhat but we find no indication that television was more likely than print media to ignore foreign stories. On a percentage basis, it is the magazine news coverage that seems to give foreign affairs short shrift. Our study is not designed as a large-scale comparative content analysis, so we are not in a position to make grand judgments of relative emphasis among the different media. But from the evidence at hand, the coverage is roughly equivalent. The exceptions are the low level of newsmagazine coverage of South Africa and SDI and network television's modest coverage of the stock market crash.

Overall Differences in Media Coverage

Other patterns of differential news coverage are described in table 3.4. We begin our analysis with a note about the hazards of any comparison across media. As the pundits frequently remark, all of the words spoken in a typical evening newscast (consisting of about twenty-two and a half minutes of actual news) would not fill the front page of a newspaper.

Table 3.4 reveals that the word count for the average newspaper article is roughly twice that for the average television story, and the average magazine story is well over three times as long. To enhance the comparability of the data, we have accordingly reported the results two ways: first, in terms of the actual length of stories (which gives a certain advantage to newspaper and especially magazine stories, both of which tend to have a larger number of words than television stories), and second, per-100-words (i.e., controlling for different average story lengths). We consider the per-word results an indicator of information density.

Table 3.4 tells two stories. The top half of the table reveals a net advantage to newsmagazine coverage along two dimensions of learning. The extra space and much higher average word count make room for more personalized as well as more contextual information in newsmagazines. While all of the media tend to cover possible causes and consequences of issues, the mean number of statements about causes and consequences of issues for magazine stories is approximately

Table 3.4   Media Emphasis on Human Interest and Political Context

	TV	Magazine	Newspaper
Overall Average Per Story			
Average story length in words**	360	1,182	641
Attention/involvement factors:			
No. of visual images**	24.1	2.0	0.4
Human interest reference	1.2	1.6	1.0
Specific person reference**	6.0	11.8	7.7
Context factors:			
Expert sources*	4.2	8.5	6.0
Causes**	3.1	7.6	4.1
Consequences**	4.2	13.2	6.3
Definitions**	0.7	2.1	0.9
Policy references**	2.5	5.8	3.2
Per 100 Words Average			
Attention/involvement factors:			
No. of pictures**	6.7	0.2	0.1
Human interest**	0.4	0.2	0.2
References to specific people*	2.2	1.3	1.3
Context factors:			
Expert sources	1.1	0.8	1.2
Causes	0.9	0.8	0.7
Consequences	1.3	1.2	1.1
Definitions	0.3	0.2	0.2
Policy references*	0.9	0.6	0.6

**F significant at .01.
*F significant at .05.

twice as great as the means for the other media in every contextual category (e.g., definitions or policy alternatives). The media are often criticized for trivializing the news by ignoring the historical and economic context of political issues (Marcuse, 1964; Bennett, 1988; Habermas, 1989 [1962]). Our content analysis does not support the assertion that there is no context for news, but clearly magazines provide more context than other news outlets.

While magazines provide more contextual information, television naturally has the advantage in pictorial and graphic information, with approximately twenty-four different camera cuts in an average 2.25-minute story. The lower half of table 3.4 reports per-word measures of information density. Here, the advantage tips in favor of broadcast journalism, especially on the elements of the news that might be associated with audience attention or involvement. When controlling for the length of stories, television news refers to more people in its news presentations than do either newspapers or magazines. The table shows on average almost twice as many human interest examples and twice as many references to specific people per 100 words on television than for either of the other media. The results confirm that television is not only the most densely packed medium in terms of visuals, but the most personalized medium as well.

The Structural Syntax of News Stories in the Different Media

We also examined the structure of news presentation in different media, on the assumption that the order of the presentation might have an important impact on the audience's ability to learn, understand, and recall information from the news. We looked at when and to what extent various story elements were introduced: the framing of the story, the factual information, analysis, and expressions of affect and opinion.

Each story used in our learning experiments was coded, phrase by phrase, into several structural content categories. In the analysis reported below, "framing" of the news stories covers statements of the problem, the setting of the story in time, and moral prognostications.[3] "Facts" include statements of verifiable information about events, people, places, or objects. "Analysis" refers to explanations of cause and effect, definitions and examples of each issue as well as predictions and statements about possible outcomes of policy alternatives. "Opinions" measure expressions of affect and particular points of view on the issues. If a phrase contained both opinion and fact, it was coded in both categories. The stories varied in length and in the number of codes. In order to make comparisons across media, length was controlled by setting all stories equal to 100 codes.

Figure 3.1 shows that the structures of the stories vary in terms of presentational order. Television devotes approximately 45 percent of its initial coverage to framing the issue, but then framing falls off sharply. The high rate of framing at the very beginning of the TV sto-

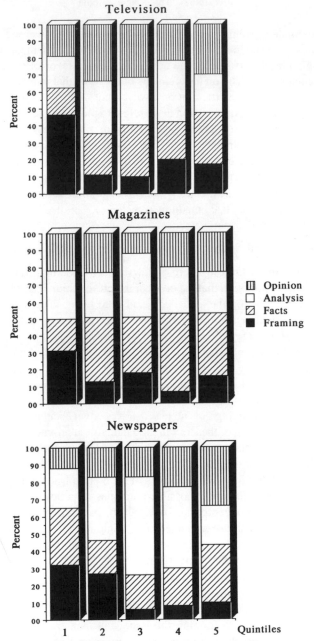

Figure 3.1 A Comparison of Story Structure in the Three Media

ries is due in part to the typical practice of having the anchor introduce the story, followed by a cut to the reporter on the scene who sets up the story again. While magazines and newspapers also frame issues early in the stories, opinions are presented earlier in newsmagazines, while facts appear earlier in newspapers. For example, the average number of facts presented in the first 20 percent of the story is 7.4 for newspapers, 4.7 for television, and 3.2 for magazines. In other words, almost 60 percent of the first quintile of newspaper stories is devoted to factual statements. Television and magazines never achieve as high a percentage and tend to present facts later in their coverage. In analyzing the structural syntax of news stories, we note that it is difficult to differentiate among statements of fact, analysis, and opinion. Reporters are quite adept at combining several of these elements into a single sentence or expression. This combination of syntactical techniques may confound the audience or, as Edelman has argued, may provide ambiguous messages for the construction of political meaning (Edelman, 1988).

Audience Evaluations of the Three News Media

The objective analysis of words and symbols in news content tells us only what is potentially available to people but not necessarily what they are processing or learning. Audience perceptions can only be inferred from the standard content analysis. The aim of our audience evaluations of news content is to provide a means of assessing the actual subjective responses to presentational aspects of news stories which we suspect are essential to the learning from the news media. We hoped to establish whether or not the audience perceived the media differences revealed by objective coding and, further, whether we could identify differences in the way people responded to news presentations that objective coding could not measure.

Audience judges were asked to evaluate news stories on a number of entertainment and expository dimensions of news presentation. We drew the ninety judges from the same population as our experimental subjects. We asked the evaluators to rate each news story on a number of factors which previous research (Gunter, 1987; Robinson and Levy, 1986; Graber, 1988) suggested might be related to learning from the news media and which overlapped with the content analysis conducted by trained coders. In particular, subjects were asked whether stories excited their attention, were visually interesting, were easy to understand, were factual, or provided a relevant context for news.

Television, of course, is the most intensely visual medium, while newspapers and magazines have the benefit of more "space" for providing facts and context. The evaluations of the mass audience coders, presented in table 3.5, reflect these familiar patterns. Stories in the print media were judged as providing a greater amount of contextual information than television stories. Audience evaluators rated magazines high on political, historical, and economic contextualization as well as on ideas about what people can do about the issues. Newspaper coverage was viewed as the most factual, while television was generally viewed as providing the least contextual information (although in many cases, the differences were not statistically significant). In addition, the evaluators demonstrated the extent to which audience involvement varied significantly by medium.

Over all of the issues, television coverage was consistently evaluated as more attention-grabbing, interesting, personally relevant, emotionally involving, and surprising than newspaper or magazine coverage. The audience reported a greater sense of attachment to the issues when they were presented by television than when they were

Table 3.5   Audience Evaluations of the Three Media
(Means from 7-Point Scales for All Issues)

	TV	Magazine	Newspaper
Involving:			
Grab attention**	5.3	4.8	4.5
Emotional*	4.8	4.4	4.1
Surprising**	4.6	3.9	3.3
Vividness**	5.2	3.1	2.9
Pictures enhance story**	5.5	3.0	2.8
Personally relevant	4.3	4.0	3.7
Contextual:			
History**	3.1	4.1	3.6
Economics**	3.6	4.4	4.3
Causes	4.3	4.6	4.9
Effects	5.0	4.8	5.0
What people can do**	2.4	3.3	2.6

**F significant at .01.
*F significant at .05.

reported by newspapers or magazines. Since the highly visual character of television is an obvious attribute that may account for these affective differences, we explored this dimension separately (Graber, 1987).

The Visual Element

Not surprisingly, our non-expert audience judges found that television stories were more "visual" than those in magazines and newspapers. It is not clear, however, what impact the visuals have on the typical viewer. Previous research has supported both sides of the visual debate. Some find that television's use of pictures is conducive to learning. Pictures attract the attention of the audience and may be used to augment the verbal messages, enhancing recall and learning from the news story (Lang and Lang, 1953; Lanzetta et al., 1985; Alger, 1987; Graber, 1987; Kern, 1989). Others find that visuals contradict or distract attention from the verbal message so as to confuse or disengage the viewer (Robinson and Levy, 1986). Or, the visuals may overwhelm and numb the audience (Milburn and McGrail, 1990).

Our objective coding of the news presentations demonstrates that television far outstrips magazines and newspapers in the use of pictures. Overall, the television coverage used in our experiments contained at least four times the number of visuals than either the magazine or newspaper stories. For example, the televised version of the SDI story on public relations commercials contained a continuously running video of the advertisements interspersed with quick shots of talking heads, Madison Avenue, and children. In contrast, the magazine used two color photographs taken from pro- and anti-Star Wars commercials. The newspaper coverage contained a six-panel black and white cartoon peopled with stick figures trying to avoid being hit by nuclear missiles while commenting ironically about the pot of gold at the end of the Star Wars rainbow.

Surprisingly often, the visuals that were used in the magazine stories were in the television stories as well. For example, magazine and television stories about apartheid in South Africa contained identical pictures of a van being overturned on a street in the Cape Town suburb of Athlone. Even less event-centered stories employed some of the same visuals. Magazine and television coverage of children born addicted to cocaine contained interviews and pictures of the same UCLA doctor holding a "cocaine baby." The newspaper story, on the other hand, did not use any photographs and interviewed doctors in Chicago and Boston. While it is true that the stories we used in our learning experiments were selected to be as similar as possible, the use of identical visuals by television and magazines seems to give further credence to the concept of pack journalism, or rather pack photography.

As expected, audience evaluators not only reported that television stories were more visual but also judged those visuals as significantly more vivid than the pictures or graphics used in either of the print media. Although the stories varied in the quantity and character of their visuals, the evaluators insisted that television's more vivid pictures enhanced their understanding regardless of the topic. In response to the question, "Did the pictures/graphics help you to understand the story?," the average response was 2.8 and 3.0, respectively, on a 7-point scale for newspaper and magazine stories. The mean rating for television, however, was at the other end of the scale at 5.5. There is no doubt that the visual images used by television are noticed and appreciated by the audience. As one of our respondents said when talking about South Africa: "Television is good for, if something is really ugly. Taking a picture of it and, say, well this is what we've been telling you about. Here's a picture of it—all in motion, technicolor motion, holy mackerel!"

In a study reported elsewhere (Crigler, Just, and Neuman, 1991), we did not find, however, that television visuals (by themselves) were especially effective in conveying information or evoking an affective response within the audience. Rather it is a combination of the audio track and the visual imagery of television that produces a strong impact.

Different Media, Different Strengths

Our analysis of media coverage of the five issues has provided evidence for possible advantages in learning from each of the three media. The analysis of the contextualization of news indicates that coverage in weekly newsmagazines contains a greater number of contextual and expository elements than either of the other media. On average, the longer magazine stories include more references to expert sources, definitions of terms and concepts, and more analysis of the causes, consequences, and possible policy outcomes of the issues than either television or newspaper coverage. A hypothesis about learning that favors magazines would be that people learn more from magazine coverage of political issues because readers are provided with more contextual information.

Although magazine stories provide a broad context, they are longer than either television or newspaper stories and use far fewer visual images than television. In fact, if we control for the length of the story or the use of pictures, the advantages of magazine contextualization disappear. Here, the advantages lie with television coverage. Television stories are densely packed and highly visual. In addition, the audience evaluators rated television coverage as more attention-grabbing, emotional, surprising, interesting, and personally relevant than coverage by either print medium. A competing television hypothesis about learning would be that television is the most effective medium for helping individuals understand political issues, because of the attraction and involvement provided by fast pacing and visuals.

On the basis of our objective analysis of news stories, we could also hazard a newspaper hypothesis. Clearly newspaper coverage is neither as visual as television nor as rich in contextual information as magazines. The analysis of the structural syntax of the three media, however, indicates that newspapers emphasize facts early in the story. This is in accordance with the inverted pyramid structure hailed in journalism textbooks of the 1950s. The inverted pyramid is easy to read and store because the vital information is presented early and certainly before the text jumps to subsequent pages. Newspapers, then, might be the most effective medium for learning about political issues, because they organize information early in the story.

Chapters 5 and 6 test these competing media hypotheses. We ask just how well these different news story structures work when it comes to learning from news. We turn first, however, to an analysis of media framing of the news stories and how those patterns match up with the mass public's construction of the same issues.

FOUR
Making Sense of the News

In seeking to make sense of the political world, both the media and the public employ simplifying cognitive frames as hooks to capture a piece of the abundant flow of confusing and conflicting information from Lippmann's "world outside." In this chapter we identify five predominant conceptual frames which are evident in both media coverage and informal public discourse about politics. The typology was developed independently but turns out to be similar to other analytic schemes of news framing.[1] Our examination of the way individuals conceptualize public issues reveals a complex process in which meaning is constructed from diverse personal and mediated experiences (Crigler and Jensen, 1991). We find that people are adept at drawing emotional and moral lessons from the rather dry style of "objective" public discourse prevalent in the American media (Marcus and Rahn, 1990).

Framing Political Discourse

Frames are conceptual tools which media and individuals rely on to convey, interpret, and evaluate information. We use the term frame rather than schema, script, or cognitive structure (Lau and Sears, 1986; Graber, 1988; Rosenberg, 1988) because the latter terms refer primarily to individuals' structures of thought and often imply a deterministic or hierarchical structure of information and ideas within the mind. Most analyses of framing issues in the news have focused on the media with a (most often brief) look at audience interpretations (Cohen, 1963; Galtung and Ruge, 1965; Altheide, 1976; Gans, 1979; Glasgow University Media Group, 1976, 1980; Tuchman, 1978; Cohen and Young, 1981; Lang and Lang, 1983; Robinson and Sheehan, 1983; Manoff and Schudson, 1986; Bennett, 1988; van

Dijk, 1988). Following Graber (1988) and Gamson (1989, 1992), we started first with the audience and derived our typology and analysis of issue frames from the depth interviews and then turned to a parallel content analysis of media coverage for a comparative analysis.

To illustrate the dynamic character of issue framing, one might revisit the classic theories of cognitive dissonance, selective exposure, and balance theory (Festinger, 1957; Heider, 1958; Freedman and Sears, 1965). In these theories the individual is defined as having a set of clear-cut opinions on an issue or set of issues that "determine" which new information the individual will permit to cross his or her cognitive threshold. It certainly seemed to make sense that people were not equally open or attentive to every possible fragment of information or opinion in their environment. In empirical tests, especially with broadcast news, these theories of self-protection did not survive well (Insko, 1984; Frey, 1986). There is indeed ample evidence of selective patterns of attention, but the key concept is not opinion-protection, but a somewhat more complex phenomenon of interpretation and meaning construction. The frame does not predetermine the information individuals will seek but it may shape aspects of the world that the individual experiences either directly or through the news media and is thus central to the process of constructing meaning.

We identified the frames for the issues we examined from an analysis of in-depth interviews conducted with a small number of experimental subjects. There were forty-eight loosely structured, oral interviews. Each interviewer was prepared with six general questions to stimulate discussion, and was instructed to probe and follow up on ideas mentioned by the interviewee in a nondirective manner (see Appendix for probe questions and an excerpt from a sample interview). Emphasis was placed on the individual's structuring of issues and opinions, rather than on the individual's fitting of views to an interviewer's questions, expectations, or possible response categories (Mishler, 1986). The goal of these interviews was to elicit information from people "in their own voices" rather than to emphasize the replicability of a structured interview. This approach was seen as especially appropriate for the examination of political understanding.

The central role of conceptual frames became clear from analysis of the interviews and media stories. At the outset, we were simply exploring how issues were presented and interpreted, but in short order it became evident that both individuals and the media draw heavily on a few central frames for interpreting all five public issues. The most pronounced frames involved economic themes, divisions of protagonists into "us" and "them," perceptions of control by powerful others, a sense of the human impact of issues, and the application of moral values. It is important to note that people use multiple frames to discuss each political issue. While some frames were more often evident for certain issues, the selection of an issue does not determine the frame to be used.

One conceptual frame notably missing from the natural discourse about issues was the liberal-conservative continuum. We confirm the frequently reported finding that this conceptual mainstay of political science and professional politics is seldom employed in the informal discourse of the mass citizenry (Converse, 1964; Lane, 1973; Neuman, 1986).

The frames we found, however, functioned in much the same way that the liberal-conservative continuum was thought to operate. They helped subjects to determine the personal relevance of the issues, to provide linkages among issues, and to formulate arguments from which opinions could be drawn. Interestingly, however, opinion positions could not be inferred directly from the use of particular issue frames. People who use an economic frame, for example, do not all share the same pro- or anti-SDI opinions; their support or rejection of SDI was simply based on what were primarily economic arguments. Similarly, people who use the conflict frame for Star Wars might identify the United States as "us" and the Soviet Union as "them," but others might identify "them" as the Reagan Administration, and "us" as citizens helpless to influence Reagan's policies.

In our analysis we also examined the media use of framing and found there too a lack of a determining connection between frames and the political positions of political spokespersons even though frames channel discourse in important ways in the press (Iyengar and Kinder, 1987; Iyengar, 1991). Below we explore the divergent uses of common frames by the media and the audience. It soon becomes clear that in their active interpretation of the political world, audience members alternatively accept, ignore, and reinterpret the dominant frames offered by the media.

The Economic Frame

Both the news media and individuals apply the economic frame to a broad range of issues (Barkin and Gurevitch, 1987). The economic frame reflects the preoccupation with "the bottom line," profit and loss, and wider values of the culture of capitalism. The media tend to employ technical language for the economic frame, while people are far more likely to overlay the frame with a moral or evaluative dimension. The economic frame fits well with the media's propensity to cover news from the standpoint of official sources (Sigal, 1973). Media stories frequently covered the costs of government programs and the economic consequences of pursuing or not pursuing various policy objectives. SDI, drug abuse, and AIDS stories included dollar estimates of costs for government programs that had come from various official sources. The *Boston Globe,* for example, reported that "Reagan's $3.7 billion funding request for the 'Star Wars' program in the current fiscal year has been trimmed by approximately $1 billion."

Media discussion of the stock market crash was the issue most frequently framed in economic terms. A *Boston Globe* story, for instance, reported thus: "With yesterday's decline added in, the total paper loss could exceed $1 trillion." In spite of the huge dollar figures involved, the media's use of the economic frame is often abstract and technical. In a story that was subtitled "How America's Budget and Trade Deficits Grew to Daunting Heights," one newsmagazine article explained the causes of the crash in relation to more than a dozen economic concerns, including the following: the budget and trade deficits, taxes, pork-barrel legislation, defense spending, "voodoo" Reaganomics, supply side tax cuts, user fees, Social Security, farm supports, Gramm-Rudman deficit reduction, the Federal Reserve, and declining currency values. The focus was on governmental actions and rather technical economic questions.

Approximately half of our interviewees framed at least one issue in economic terms but they tended to put a human face on it. The media's numbers are reflected back as human impact, values, or moral judgments. As one woman remarked about SDI, "I don't know much about the technology, but it's expensive . . . But, to me, even if it's expensive, I just as soon pay taxes for it, if it would help, if it was something that would help us." Another interviewee, a self-employed engineer in his mid-fifties, used an economic frame but with a highly moral tone applied to the issue of apartheid in South Africa. He said:

> It's absolutely atrocious. I think the supremacists in South
> Africa ought to be done away with as completely as possible
> . . . Blow the ship out of the water. Whatever it takes and I

don't think we ought to waste money on throwing them in
jail. I think it's a waste of resources.

Greed was seen as motivating various actions by governments and
individuals. In fact, profit motives were mentioned in discussions of
SDI, apartheid, and drug abuse, but not AIDS. Often, individuals saw
the profits going to powerful others who could not always be trusted.
A retired woman in her early sixties mentioned the futility of trying to
fight against the powerful others in and around government. "You
can't get at those, uh, the big money people. You cannot get at those
big money people. This is something we all talk about—all these big
issues, but, uh, when it comes right down to it, there's just a few that
have a, a lotta say."

Interestingly, our interviewees also included the media among the
powerful others motivated by greed. Several of them employed an
economic frame to suggest that the media's main concern in issue
coverage was ratings or profits. A secretary in her early fifties noted:

> I just think that they [the media] want to make a buck. You
> know? It's behind most everything, anyway, as far as hype
> goes. Selling something . . . So, they want to get the mass
> population watching their show, which is what they have to
> do, in order to appease their sponsor, who pays a lot of
> money, and this is a very interesting topic.

On the whole, while the application of the economic frame by the
media tended to reinforce dominant capitalist social values and to emphasize the abstract and technical aspects of the economy, individuals
used the economic frame to draw moral lessons about human behavior, particularly greed.

The Conflict Frame

The communications literature is rife with references to the media's
emphasis on conflict as a means of attracting attention and readership.
Polarized forces—"the two sides of the issue," "horse-race politics"
—are dominant themes identified with the presentation of news. The
conflict frame fits well with the media's game interpretation of the political world as an ongoing series of contests, each with a new set of
winners and losers (Crouse, 1973; Gans, 1979; Patterson, 1980). In
fact the received definition of good journalistic practice emphasizes

reporting stories in terms of experts who offer clashing interpretations (McDougall, 1968; Green, 1969; Brooks et al., 1985). In covering the South Africa story, for example, the media cited many different polarized forces including these: blacks vs. whites, blacks vs. police, the South African government vs. journalists, and South Africa vs. the rest of the world. Dan Rather's lead-in to a story typifies the latter frame: "South Africa today turned a defiant deaf ear to worldwide calls for clemency and hanged a twenty-eight-year-old black poet for killing a policeman."

In another example, this from a television story, the media use two sets of polarized forces—the United States and the Soviet Union, and pro- and anti-Star Wars groups within the United States.

> As the U.S. and the Soviet Union fence over the implications of the space-based defenses at the arms control talks in Geneva, proponents and opponents of Reagan's Strategic Defense Initiative are vying for the allegiance of the American public. On college campuses and television screens, in board rooms and scientific symposiums, the two sides are intent on persuading Americans that Star Wars is either (a) an impossible and dangerous dream or (b) the ultimate nuclear umbrella.

Our respondents also use a conflict frame in their discussion of the five issues, but much less often than the media. Perhaps the most dramatic use of a polarized us/them frame by individuals occurs on the topic of race and racism. In reference to the South Africa question, for example, this woman brings up racial relations in the United States in a highly polarized fashion.

> But, I think most Americans, including myself, I don't look down on the blacks. I don't feel superior to them, but I don't want to mingle with them. I don't mind if I work with them, but I don't want any of my kids to marry one of them. And, I don't particularly want to socialize with them. And, this country here, they want to push immediately, immediate equality in South Africa. And it can't be done.

Gamson (1992) finds similar patterns in his group interviews concerning affirmative action. Overt racism like this was not evident in the media coverage, but persists with disturbing frequency in the depth interviews.

Individuals also utilize an us/them conflict frame to voice suspicion of other countries's motives in the area of international relations.[2] This became evident in the discussions of SDI. For instance, a retired man described the Russians in what might be characterized as a canonical Cold War conflict frame.

> As far as Star Wars, it sounds good. The fear that comes from, well Russia is the one who has the great fear, and it's understandable. They fear that it could be employed as an offensive weapon, see. I think, perhaps, that comes from because of their own nature, you see, myself, I don't have a very high opinion of communistic government. I think with every move they make is done to gain something, to gain an advantage, or put somebody at a disadvantage and so, I think perhaps, they suspect us of the same thing.

But we find ample evidence of oppositional readings of Cold War ideology among our respondents in 1987, well before the dramatic shifts in Soviet military and diplomatic posture. One man, for example, uses an us/them frame to discuss SDI, but felt that the Russians are like him and want peace. However, he is not completely sure; in fact, he is "in definite doubt."

> I really believe that Russia really and truly wants peace as much as I do. And, the average Russian person doesn't want to kill the average American person . . . And, I can't see why this country can't learn to co-exist . . . that's how I feel, right, I could be 100 percent wrong. That's because I'm in definite doubt . . . I mean, I don't think they want to kill me.

Journalistic tradition, which emphasizes telling "both sides of the story" and the impulse to put together an interesting narrative, if possible with good guys and bad guys, leads to a heavy media emphasis on forces in conflict. The framing of issues in the mass public includes the conflict frame but uses it less often. When it is used, it is more often in personalized terms of "people like me" versus other social groups or more generalized "powerful others."

The Powerlessness Frame

Literature in communications and politics has taken issue with the media for not being critical enough of those who are in power, especially government and corporate elites (Gitlin, 1980; Bennett, 1988; Entman, 1989). We found evidence to support this view, but we also found examples in which the media described officials and other powerful individuals as helpless in the face of greater forces—that is, government as victim. The stories on apartheid in South Africa at times portrayed the powerlessness of blacks or journalists against the repressive and powerful South African government, but at other times, the stories viewed the situation as a tide of powerful black dissent that was spreading inevitably across South Africa and threatening the white minority and its government. A television reporter gave the following oral commentary as video of clashing blacks and whites was being broadcast.

> The defiance spilled onto the streets. When police first attempted to break up the demonstration, blacks fought back. Two policemen were injured, one seriously. The police then seemed unwilling or unable to control the crowd. Suddenly, whites in the center of Johannesburg began to experience the anger and violence that until now has been largely contained in the black townships. Passing whites were taunted and chased. The windows of white-owned shops were smashed and looted. At times, the police seemed helpless, running from the black onslaught.

Powerlessness was essential to the stories about AIDS. AIDS was covered in the media as an epidemic and spreading beyond anyone's immediate control. "The NAS panel's greatest worry is that the virus is being spread further every day and largely by people who may not know they have it . . . Little if anything can be done to help those who are now infected and will fall sick over the next five years." The *Time* story later quotes the Public Health Service to warn people that AIDS can infect anyone: " 'This virus does not discriminate by sex, age, race, ethnic group or sexual orientation.' "

The media use the powerlessness frame to express the dominance of forces (e.g., the stock market, the deadly AIDS virus, the power of cocaine addiction) over weak individuals or groups (e.g., South African blacks and AIDS victims). Again, because the media are reporting other people's stories, control (or lack thereof) is expressed not from an individual's perspective, but from the perspective of a more objective third person.

The powerlessness frame was evident in approximately half of the interviews and was used more frequently by women than by men. Three-quarters of the interviewees who used the powerlessness frame were women. For most of the people who used the frame, the issue of lack of control was evident throughout the interview. For a number of others, however, it was present only in their discussions of drug abuse.

The concept of "powerful others" in control, of course, is central to the "locus of control" concept in social psychology.[3] In our interviews, the powerful others identified in the frame included the government, Ronald Reagan, the "wealthy and well-connected," computers, and God. For example, a middle-aged postal employee spoke about Ronald Reagan as the driving force behind SDI.

> I think it's just an idea that Reagan has planned up in his head and I think he's gonna go ahead on it, and the public be damned and everything else be damned, just like Bork . . . I don't think Reagan can accept a negative position from the American people, or anything. I think he's gotta have it. We're gonna have it, because he wants it. He's gonna ram it right down our throats.

The American government is not the only controlling force. One female respondent, when talking about the situation in South Africa, said: "The [South African] government is really—I see it as a gigantic foot, just stepping on them and keeping them down."

Some people emphasized the power of inanimate forces. Computers "out of control" were seen as an important factor in triggering the stock market crash. A middle-aged realtor said, "What happened that day [pause], it happened mostly because of the way computers were running, because people do not sell that much stock on one day . . . Most money was lost and it was because I think computers just said 'sell, sell, sell,' and everything was sold."

A religiously oriented deference to powerful natural forces was especially prominent with regard to the AIDS issue. A young woman employed as a bookkeeper said that "someone told me once that it's God's way of controlling the population. If they control AIDS, He's just going to throw something else out, so it's never going to end." A teacher, emphasizing the mysteries of life notes:

> It's going to happen eventually. Nostradamos or Notradamos—whatever his name is—says by the year such and

such, we're gonna be gone. Hopefully, by the year such and such I won't be around and my grandchildren won't be around and my great-grandchildren won't be around. I think it's out of control. It's out of my control, I know that. If it's gonna happen, it's gonna happen. So I think a lot of people think like I do. There's nothing we can do about it, so let's not dwell on the subject . . . When it happens, it happens. We'll see. If I'm dead, I'm dead. If I'm bald, I'm bald.

Closely tied with these beliefs in powerful others and fate were feelings of little personal control over the course of events or policy decisions about these issues. One young woman, when talking about SDI, said: "Somebody higher has the control over this [SDI]. We don't have any control. We can vote for things, but um, vote for the nuclear arms to stop. I signed a petition yesterday for, ah, to stop nuclear waste dumps. And that's about all we can do as the little people." A forty-six-year-old receptionist felt frustrated about the situation in South Africa. "I get upset because I feel absolutely helpless to know these things are going on and I can't fix them." Another woman expressed an inability to effect any change in the drug abuse problem. "Just you and I, a lay person, what are . . . what are we going to do?"

The Human Impact Frame

The media's use of the human impact frame focuses on describing individuals and groups who are likely to be affected by an issue. The official voice of the journalist, however, avoids direct expression of compassion for the people involved. Rather, it seems that reporters put a "human face" on stories by providing human examples and exemplars (Mencher, 1984). In contrast, the individuals who employ a human impact frame express their personal concerns and compassion with a visceral directness.

All three media used the hanging of poet and African National Congress member, Benjamin Moloise, as a personification of the conditions of apartheid. While the media stories used in our experiments did not explicitly frame stories in empathetic or compassionate terms, they did employ adjectives, personal vignettes, and visuals that might generate feelings of outrage, empathy, sympathy, or compassion from their audiences. For example, a television story on the effects of cocaine use during pregnancy told the story of one young child who had been taken from her mother and placed in a foster home. The video shows a view of the foster parents trying to help the little girl sit on her own in their living room. Part way through the story, the camera pans back so that we can also see another child playing and drinking milk out of a cup while she is standing in front of the cocaine-affected child.

> FOSTER MOTHER: "She has no sense of balance. As you can see when we sit her up, she will fall either forwards, backwards, or to the side."

> REPORTER: "She cannot crawl. A neighbor child, Miriam, is exactly the same age but normal and developing. The cocaine youngster with her bottle."

> FOSTER FATHER: "She just forgets that she likes that milk. Her brain just doesn't transmit that to her. She just drops the bottle and then she'll cry."

> REPORTER: "Miriam can drink from a cup. What's ahead for her playmate?"

Often, these tales of human impact were used to illustrate that a situation was a problem deserving the audience's attention. The media, however, tended to avoid direct expressions of emotions or evaluative statements. Because of the powerful media norms of objectivity, emotions were usually reserved for news sources. The only time direct feelings of compassion worked their way into the stimulus stories was when a person was being interviewed or quoted, although this did not occur often. We did find, in a magazine story on AIDS, emotional comments by a counselor who daily saw the anguish of couples undergoing the AIDS tests.

> "The test tends to rip people's lives apart," says Dooley Worth, who leads a support group of high risk women, many of them former intravenous drug users in Manhattan. "I've even seen couples who are both negative break up because of questions raised from just getting the test."

This woman's discussion reports that couples may be "ripped apart," but there is no explicit expression of sorrow, pity, or empathy. Thus, unlike our individual interviewees who freely emoted as they described political issues using the human impact frame, the media's frame was more limited to a reporting of events that impacted people.

Interviewees were even more likely than the media to discuss issues in terms of the effects they have on people. Most often those who used human impact frames justified opinions by arguing that the issue in question either "hurt" or "helped" people. Expressions of concern for one's self and family and the effects of an issue on the individual's immediate circle of acquaintance were seen in most of the interviews. One man drew a particularly narrow circle around himself, claiming not to be interested in knowing anything about drug abuse because it did not affect him or anyone he knows. Drug abuse is not a salient topic for him. "I don't know much about it because I don't feel concerned with it [drugs] in the sense that it doesn't in any way directly affect me. As I say, I don't know a single person who uses it, at least that let's me know that they use it. I never did."

Individuals more often widened the scope of the impact to include friends and community. A housewife in her mid-thirties identifies very closely with her town and issues that affect that sphere.

> We have a strong issue right now running in my community that's taking up a lot of time . . . To me, my community is more important than the world. OK, I mean, I have to live in this community. I have to live in the world, but it's so big, and my community is so small. Where I have to live in that community, where it affects me personally, then it is something that I should do about it.

We found that people frequently express concern for others with whom they do not identify, as well as for those with whom they do. Thus, the human impact frame was often marked by feelings of caring, worry, and compassion for others. People were able to use their imaginations to put themselves in someone else's shoes. A few of our interviewees were able to empathize with other groups to such a great extent that the distinguishing lines between the in-groups and others disappeared altogether. These people tended to evaluate issues based on their impact on human beings in general. They spoke in compassionate terms about the human condition as a whole. For example, a retired man in his late sixties said:

> Well, any time any human being gets hurt, I feel bad about it, it's important. I mean, a human being should come first in everything. You worry about drugs, you worry about AIDS, you worry about SDI because of the money that's spent and

it's not being spent on the people that need it. You worry
about all these things because it's human beings behind it
that's being affected by it.

Individuals' use of the human impact frame demonstrates that
people are able to empathize with people and situations well beyond
their immediate experience. The media emphasize human impact stories as a natural technique to lure in the attention of their audiences.
Newscasters and print reporters, of course, do not express empathy or
compassion overtly but rely on their sources and the victims themselves to tell their stories with the full emotional force a participant is
likely to convey.

The Morality Frame

The professional norm of "objectivity" in journalism has been with us
for so many years it is taken for granted by journalist and audience
member alike. Schudson's illuminating historical analysis of how that
norm evolved (1978) reminds us not only that a century ago norms
were very different but also that such norms are culturally and eco-
nomically derived. Of all the content analyses of media framing cited
above, none would dispute that cultural values are deeply embedded
in modern journalistic practice. References to moral values in the media are simply more indirect than, for example, what we find in the
mass audience depth interviews.

While our respondents might condemn the "sinners" who got AIDS
with some vehemence, the media make reference to such a moral
frame indirectly through quotation or inference. As with expressions
of empathy in the human impact frame, reporters, for the most part,
are not in a position to speak directly and have to find someone else to
"raise the issue." For example, *Time* used the views of the Roman
Catholic church to raise the question of the morality of sexual education. "In the view of the Roman Catholic Church, for example, a Government campaign to urge use of condoms would be encouraging
people to commit mortal sin. The church regards condoms as artificial
contraceptive devices whose use, even to avoid lethal disease, is for-
bidden."

The *Boston Globe* ended a story on cocaine and pregnancy with a
moral directive issued to pregnant women by a doctor. "Don't use cocaine. And if you have used it, make sure to tell your physician." The

television story on cocaine babies ended on a very moralistic and condemning tone. The future and past of the young foster child who could not even sit without help were juxtaposed to send a message to the audience.

> FOSTER MOTHER: She may in fact be a twenty-one-year-old with an IQ of perhaps 50, barely able to dress herself and probably unable to live alone.

> REPORTER: Her mother told authorities that she was just a recreational cocaine user. Terry Drinkwater, CBS News, Malibu.

In contrast to moralizing in the media, virtually all of the interviewees used moral and value-laden statements to talk about the five political issues. Public discourse, unlike media discourse, employed many references to morality, God and other religious tenets, and values such as equality, freedom, and peace. All of the issues were discussed by individuals in these terms, although some of the strongest moral language was used with AIDS. One man said that homosexuality is "against the law of man. It's against the law of God." Several other people echoed this view, as one woman suggested, "It can be snuffed out if everybody lived by the ten commandments." Perhaps AIDS was God's punishment, a modern-day plague. "I think that the good Lord is doing this to stop all the living—the way people are living today," said one sixty-five-year-old man. A woman admitted, "I think that, I hate to say this, but maybe God decided to bring it to scare people with their loose morals." One woman argued that there might be some good to come from AIDS. "I think our morals might build a little, you know, because people have been very free. I'm not one of those people who have been very free, so I'm for this, you know. I don't know why it [AIDS] happened, but in a way it's good. It's a good thing it did, because people's ideas have changed."

Peace, love, and the "golden rule" were also expressed when one receptionist spoke about SDI.

> So, Star Wars, it's not my idea of anything we need. We need peace and love and understanding, trust in each other and help. We don't need it, all we need is love and companionship, getting along. Let everybody live and let live, the Golden Rule, do unto others as they do unto you.

People expressed anger about the injustices of the world and a desire for freedom, equality, and justice even if they must take the law into their own hands. In talking about apartheid in South Africa, one woman said,

> I'm appalled to see human beings [pause] like something like that goes on in our day and age . . . I just wish something could be done about it . . . I wish they would overthrow the white government and put people in there of both colors—of all colors. If they just ran the government in an equal fashion, a democratic society.

Another woman spoke about drug abuse with a great deal of compassion for children and vengefulness for drug dealers.

> My heart breaks. If I knew someone who was selling the damn drugs, I would risk going to jail for the rest of my life. I would kill him. I don't know how, I don't have a gun or anything, but I would just kill him. I would take any measure to rid the world of that kind of person [pause] selling drugs to kids.

Comparing Media Frames and Audience Frames

We have examined these five predominant frames in some detail. In each case we note both similarities and differences in the official discourse of the media and the interpretive styles of our interviewees. The relative predominance of these (or other) frames might be somewhat different had we selected other issues in the news for analysis but, we suspect, not dramatically so. At this point we step back from a micro-level analysis of the discourse itself to a broader overview of the frequency of use of the frames in the media and by the public.

A description of the relative use of each of the five frames is provided in figure 4.1. Perhaps the most dramatic difference is the heavy emphasis on conflict in the media (29 percent) compared with only 6 percent in the depth interviews. In turn, the human impact (36 percent) and moral values (15 percent) frames are more prominent in the discourse of the mass public than in the media (only 18 percent and 4 percent, respectively.)

What appears to drive these differences most strongly is tension between a news story (the recently breaking events of the day or week)

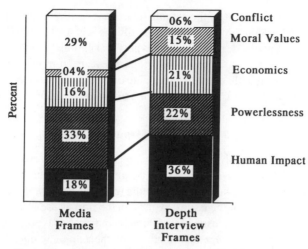

Figure 4.1   A Comparison of Image Framing: The Mass Audience
and the Mass Media

and the underlying context and enduring aspects of the news issue more broadly defined. It is the phenomenon Iyengar (1991) identifies as the "episodic" imperative of daily news coverage. Most individuals do not know much or care much about the specifics of a recent report on AIDS issued by the National Institutes of Health, but they care deeply about AIDS as a social problem, how it effects people around them and what policies ought to be put in place to respond to the epidemic. Reporting by its nature focuses on the most recent event, frequently an official press conference where experts abound and are inclined to debate (thus the heavy emphasis on the conflict theme), and not on the more personalized story of a young man or woman who succumbs to the disease.

One possible surprise, given the critical literature's emphasis on how often the media seem to reinforce the values of the established powers and champion a somewhat naive view of public participation in democratic institutions, is the media's heavy emphasis on powerlessness. This too may be derived from the episodic imperative of regularly scheduled newsmaking. The media do not shy away from chronicling the frustrations of the average citizen who confronts the medical establishment, the military establishment, or South African authorities. Nor do they avoid explaining the failures and foibles which become evident as the establishment tries with limited success to confront social problems through official channels. As Downs (1972) has illustrated, if we come to expect that national problems will be solved as quickly in the real world as they are in movies and on television, we quickly come to appreciate our powerlessness, both personally and collectively. The media bring that message home every day.

Negotiating Meaning

Our analyses of depth interviews and media coverage reveal a patterned use of a relatively few conceptual frames to discuss five divergent issues. Individuals and the media tend to use many of the same frames across each of the issues. Although the frames used by the media are similar to those used by individuals in terms of typology, they are not the same in terms of the nature of their applications. Media coverage of issues is preoccupied with covering the who, what, when, where, and (somewhat less often) the why of events. The official discourse of the media tends to be somewhat antiseptic—cleansed of much of the morality, empathy, and compassion of the political discourse of private conversations. This finding is not surprising, especially in light of the historical shift away from the partisan press of the late 1800s to the advertiser-supported mass media of today. The economic pressures to maintain the largest possible audience by alienating the fewest consumers yields a neutral, "least objectionable" style of news coverage. Moreover, the professionalization of journalism, which occurred more slowly but also started at the end of the last century, has been associated with journalistic norms of objectivity or at least intersubjectivity, removing the more highly charged political rhetoric from the news. The media's use of frames, then, echoes the constraints under which the media operate. Individuals' frames, on the other hand, are free to be richer, more affectively laden constructions of the world outside.

A long-standing debate in political communication concerns the role of conceptual frames and the level of political sophistication in the mass public. Converse, Lane, and others poured over the comments of the mass citizenry in search of the liberal-conservative continuum and found it little used. We find the same. But we do not conclude that this signifies a cognitively passive mass public. Individuals do not slavishly follow the framing of issues presented in the mass media. Rather, people frame issues in a more visceral and moralistic (and sometimes racist and xenophobic) style. They actively filter, sort, and reorganize information in personally meaningful ways in the process of constructing an understanding of public issues.

FIVE
Media Matter

While framing of issues reveals a high degree of convergence among media, our analysis of news presentation styles in Chapter 3 demonstrated significant divergence. In this chapter we return to a consideration of news presentation differences and ask: Which of the predominant news media—television, newsmagazines, or newspapers—is most likely to promote learning within the mass public? The research literature and our own content analysis suggest a number of competing hypotheses.

The dominant view is that newspapers are superior. The argument is that the traditional "inverted pyramid" structure of articles, in which the most important and most recent developments are presented in headlines and in the first few paragraphs of the story, makes newspapers an especially effective medium for learning. This view is supported by the cognitive researchers who suggest that the match between the semantic presentation of text and the storage of information in a cognitive "semantic network" may make print information easier to recall than visual information. (Rumelhart and Norman, 1985).

Weekly newsmagazines share with newspapers a text-based format but, because of their publication schedule, are able to provide a broader dimension to news—more emphasis on the historical, economic, and political context of developing news stories. If, as some researchers suggest (Graber, 1988; Bennett, 1988), contextual clues are critical to lodging information in accessible cognitive schema, then magazines may prove to be the ideal news medium for public learning.

Others, however, argue that because television is the most visual and exciting medium, it may be the most effective news tool for the mass audience. This view was confirmed by our audience evaluators who noted that television news stories grabbed and held their attention. Since the living room is not like a classroom, a news medium's ability to capture the audience's attention may be the critical element in learning from news in a natural setting.

Of the three hypotheses, the idea that television might encourage learning has historically generated the most heat, including some dramatic counterhypotheses which argue that newspapers are far superior to television in the effective presentation of news. We will explore these claims briefly before turning to the results of our learning experiments which were designed to put these competing hypotheses to the test.

Does the Medium Make a Difference?

Does the inherent character of television transform journalism and the process of political learning in the mass public? This issue, often associated with Marshall McLuhan's early work (1964), has proven to be an enduring concern in the study of political communications. Studies in the McLuhan tradition emphasize the differences in the physical modalities of video versus print and offer evidence to show that video is the most effective medium for communicating information. Sound, motion, and color attract attention and stimulate psychological involvement and ultimately learning (Chaiken and Eagly, 1976; Clarke and Fredin, 1978; Tsuneki, 1979; Drew and Reeves, 1980; Reese and Miller, 1981; Salomon and Leigh, 1984; Edwardson, Kent, and McConnell, 1985; McGuire, 1985; Brosius, 1989; Cohen, 1989; Graber, 1990). A somewhat different television hypothesis argues that the reason for television's greater effectiveness lies not so much in the modality or journalistic style of the medium, but in the minds of the beholders. Salomon, for example, summarizes his findings under the heading, "television is easy, print is tough" (Salomon, 1984). In related research, subjects report that print versions of the same information are more likely to provoke mental concentration and thought than video presentations (Wright, 1974). It is not clear that decoding television is in actuality less taxing on one's cognitive capacity than reading, for example (Reeves, Thorson, and Schleuder, 1986), but the psychological association of video with entertainment fare could critically determine how the individual thinks about the medium. Newspapers are culturally defined as a more serious enterprise.[1] Therefore, the argument goes, people may learn more from television because they *think* the information is especially accessible to them. Salomon's thesis is that because people expect television to be entertaining, they are more attentive and learn more from television than from print.

The arguments against television begin with the proposition that TV journalism is itself impoverished and that its character diminishes the political discourse in the public at large. Where the pro-television studies often rely on experimental data, studies that take an anti-television posture generally rely on analysis of the content of the medium alone or on surveys focusing on the public's reported media use. The surveys consistently find that those who depend on print sources (newspapers and magazines) for news are better informed than those who depend exclusively on television (Atkin, Galloway, and Nayman, 1976; Robinson, 1976; Patterson, 1980, Robinson and Sheehan, 1983; Robinson and Levy, 1986; Van Dijk, 1988).

The Media Experiments

To test the proposition that one news medium is more conducive to learning than another, we conducted two series of experiments (described in detail in Chapter 2 and the Appendix). In the first, or media series, we compared learning from naturally occurring stories in three news media—television, newsmagazines, and newspapers. The news coverage in each medium was carefully selected so that parallel factual information was provided for each of the five issues under study. The format of the presentation varied, of course, as is characteristic of each medium (see Chapter 3 and Appendix). The second series (the modality experiments) focused specifically on the McLuhan hypothesis and held the content of the news constant and varied only the physical modality of presentation. We used the television news stories for each issue as our source and presented audio and video, audio only, and the audio track transcribed into a simulated newspaper print format.

The Measurement of Information Gain

Our experiments are characterized by a common instrument for measuring learning from the news. We assessed the subject's information about each issue both before and after exposure to the news stories, using a simple yes/no/don't-know checklist format. For each of the five issues we identified from eleven to thirteen central elements of information which were covered in each of the three news media. We initially computed a simple learning "change score" (sometimes called a difference or gain score) for each subject, a straightforward subtraction of the number of correct answers on the pretest checklist from the post-test checklist. The resultant metric is easily understood —in our data, for example, across all five stories there was an average of 7.7 correct answers on the pretest and 8.6 correct on the post-test, for an average change score of .9, or almost one additional correct item.

But such a metric has limiting statistical properties for use in the analysis of learning (Heilizer, 1959; Rogosa, Brandt, and Zimowski, 1982). So the results reported here rely on a commonly used regression-based measure of learning which statistically controls for the subject's initial level of knowledge. Learning gain is measured by regressing the pretest score on the post-test score.[2] We recoded these "residualized change scores" and report them here as a percentage increase of the issue knowledge score in order to make a point.

We find that the average amount of "learning" from exposure to two news stories on an issue ranges from 5 to 15 percent. This metric, based on the most important factual information for each issue, draws attention to two important elements of the research. First, it demonstrates that the information gain from exposure to two stories represents a small fraction of the information in the stories themselves. Second, since the average pretest score is 65 percent (about 7 out of 11 items), learning represents as well only a small proportion of what subjects already knew about the issues. We note that, even in the experimental setting where attention levels and motivation are artificially high, learning from the news has to be understood as a gradual, incremental process.

Overall Differences in Learning

It is important to note that the design of the experiments removes several of the elements that might otherwise generate an apparent "media effect." The most important feature is the random assignment of subjects to an experimental condition. Neither the subject nor the researcher could know in advance to which kind of news the individual would be exposed. The purpose of random assignment is to make sure

that the background characteristics and interests of the subjects in each
of the learning conditions are equivalent. The media experiments hold
constant the widely noted negative association between reliance on
broadcast news and general interest in politics found in natural real-
world conditions of media exposure. In addition, this series of experiments carefully matches story content on television, newsmagazines, and newspapers to make sure that each carries the same factual
information. By choosing news stories with parallel content we hold
constant the modest, but not intangible, real-world differences in media coverage of news that we noted in Chapter 3. Given these substantial constraints which equalized the individuals in each condition as
well as the media coverage of every issue, we did not expect to find
any overall media effect. But indeed we did find one. See figure 5.1. It
contrasts dramatically with the hypothesis that those who rely on television for news will have an impoverished sense of the political world
around them.

Looking at the cumulative results from all five issues, the television
and magazine coverage resulted in significantly higher levels of learning than newspaper coverage (analysis of variance significant at $p <$
.01 level). This finding is a considerable blow to the print superiority
hypothesis and gives comfort to the view that in the era of electronic
media, television can be a useful medium for conveying conceptual
and factual information to the public. Figure 5.1 also raises questions
about the traditional assertion that newspapers by their nature are the

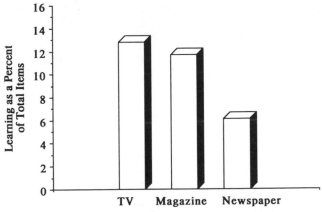

Figure 5.1   Issue Knowledge Gain by Media

superior news medium. With audiences of equal inclination toward things political, we find no evidence that broadcast journalism need be characterized as a second-class medium.

The Modality Experiments

Although we suspected that the different journalistic style and organization of news reporting was responsible for the interaction between issue and medium in our learning experiments, we wanted to explore the alternative explanation that differences in learning are due, at least in part, to the physical modality in which the news is presented, that is, on the difference between image/audio-based video and text-based print (McLuhan, 1964). Given the differences in learning between the magazine and newspaper conditions in our naturally occurring content series of experiments, we were skeptical that communications modality would prove to be a very strong explanatory factor.

Our modality experiments, like the media experiments, contrast video and print, but in this case holding the actual news content constant. Since it was impractical to create acceptable television news footage *de novo* based on printed news text, we worked the other way around and transcribed each of the television news stories and then (with very minor editing) typeset newspaper replicas. We also included an audio-only condition, simply the audio track of the original television broadcast.

We conducted modality analyses for three of the five issues (South Africa, SDI, and drugs), and the results in this case were consistent across each of the three issues. There is no significant difference in learning across the audiovisual, audio-only, and print conditions when the content is held constant, as indicated in figure 5.2. The audio condition resulted in slightly lower levels of learning, but the 2 percent difference is below levels of meaningful statistical (or theoretical) significance. These findings suggest that the differences we do find in comparing television and print media are more the result of the journalistic conventions for the presentation of news that have evolved in each medium than the physical modalities of communications by audio and moving images versus text. Marshall McLuhan's hunch, as provocative as it might be, is simply not supported by these controlled experiments. We confront a tenacious demonstration of the null hypothesis—when the differences in journalistic tradition for the pre-

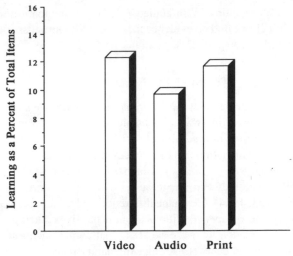

Figure 5.2   Modality Test Results

sentation of news are held constant, learning differences are not in evidence.

Attitudes toward the News Media

If the McLuhan hypothesis provides little explanation for the differences in overall learning reported in figure 5.1, perhaps we should look elsewhere. Gavriel Salomon's research on media and learning offers an interesting prospect (Salomon, 1979, 1984; Salomon and Leigh, 1984). This work argues that differences in learning from the media may be explained by differences in public expectations and attitudes (Salomon, 1984). Focusing particularly on the dramatic newspaper-TV contrasts, Salomon proposes that television is perceived primarily as an entertainment medium, featuring game shows, action adventures, and situation comedy, which happens to present news at various times of the day. Newspapers, in contrast, as a text-based medium are seen as "serious," more like a textbook or a legal document. Is the key explanatory variable for media differences to be found in the citizens' beliefs and expectations about text and video?

Salomon's work was based on Israeli school children. Other attempts to extend and test his thesis have turned up mixed results

(Beentjes and van der Voort, 1989). Although the notion that print is more "serious" and "difficult" than television has an intuitive appeal, it was not supported by our analysis of a sample of adult Americans' attitudes toward actual news and entertainment media. It appears that the mass public has no trouble at all in differentiating situation comedy from the real-world black comedy of international and national news events. In a small parallel study, we asked respondents to rank various media on four evaluative dimensions: informative, entertaining, demanding, and involving. The media included both television and a specific television news program, newspapers and a specific newspaper, magazines and a specific newsmagazine. All of the specific news sources were those actually used in our media series of experiments. Table 5.1 reports the results. We find that, although people are more likely to find television more entertaining than newspapers (87 versus 67 percent), they rate the entertainment value of specific news sources the same (47 to 53 percent). These results do not mean that people were unable to distinguish one medium from the next. They found that television in general was not "demanding" and 94 percent thought that newspapers were "informative," but when it comes to news, the results for all four dimensions were surprisingly similar, often within a few percentage points of each other. It is clear from table 5.1 that people recognize that news is work and TV news is no more expected to entertain than any other form of news.

Clearly the reason for the overall television advantage in our media experiments does not lie either in the audiovisual modality (McLuhan's hypothesis) or in the perceptions about the medium (Salomon's hypothesis). We returned, then, to our three-variable constructionist model to see if we could shed light on the results by explor-

Table 5.1 Public Perceptions of Media (%)

	Informative	Entertaining	Demanding	Involving
Television	81	87	09	70
Magazines	67	63	22	46
Newspapers	94	67	19	71
CBS News	87	47	30	60
Time Magazine	83	57	33	68
Boston Globe	80	53	27	62

ing what people learned from media about each of the issues. We suspected that there might be an interaction between the nature of the political issue at hand and the relative effectiveness of the media in communicating stories.

A Constructionist Explanation

The journalists we interviewed described what they thought were "TV-oriented" or "print-oriented" types of news stories. Their professional judgments were that concrete and immediate issues were natural for television journalism, with its film footage and on-the-spot reporting, while economic events and issues with abstract concepts and copious statistics were judged a better match for a "print piece" (Kiolbassa, 1989). The journalists led us to believe that if we separated out the results of our media series of experiments issue-by-issue, the television advantage would likely appear for the less technical, non-economic, domestic news stories, such as drug abuse and AIDS, and that print media would be more effective for learning about technical stories such as Star Wars or economic stories such as the stock market crash. When we looked at the results of the media experiments by issue, we discovered that the journalists and conventional wisdom had it backwards. This turns out to be a critical finding of our study.

Television is more successful in communicating the more abstract and distant political issues, while print media, especially newspapers, are more successful with the more immediate and concrete subject matter (see fig. 5.3). Recall that this experiment is based on naturally occurring news content. Stories were carefully selected, and each checklist was designed, so that the "raw information" called for in each checklist was covered by every medium in the experiment. What varied across media was the physical modality of communications and the stylistic differences which have evolved in each journalistic tradition.

Moving from left to right in figure 5.3 we see a complete reversal of what the conventional wisdom predicts. The relatively obscure events of South African politics and the technologically complex debate over Star Wars are more successfully communicated through television. In both issues newspapers do least well, and magazines fall between TV and newspapers; while for the human impact story of AIDS, print sources were more effective than TV. An analysis of variance of these

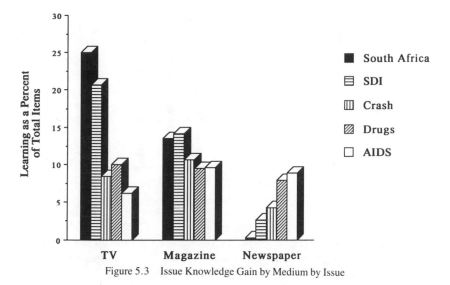

Figure 5.3   Issue Knowledge Gain by Medium by Issue

differences proves to be significant at the .05 level. There are no significant differences for the economic and drug issues.

Breaking the Attention Barrier

What could explain such a counterintuitive result? Why did television provide a better learning environment for a foreign affairs story, the considered province of newspapers? And why did a human interest story such as AIDS do so poorly in a television presentation, especially as compared to newspaper stories on the same topic? Perhaps the answer lies with the public. Among the five issues we have studied, some were clearly more important to the audience than others. It is important to keep in mind here that our sample mirrors the views expressed in national opinion polls. The salience of the five issues is distinctly ordered from the most distant/abstract issue of South Africa and Star Wars to the immediate/concrete issues of drug abuse and AIDS. Most people rated three of the issues—the economy, drug abuse, and AIDS—as "very important to me personally." But the response to Star Wars was neutral, while the importance of apartheid in South Africa for most people fell somewhere between Star Wars and the social issues.

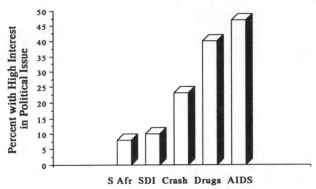

Figure 5.4   The Salience Dimension

The less salient issues tend to be ignored or overlooked when our subjects scan the media. When asked about SDI and apartheid in South Africa, one woman we interviewed replied:

> I don't know anything about that, I don't follow it [SDI]. It has to do with President Reagan, I know that and I believe it has to do with missiles and things like that, but I don't follow that. That bores me, you know what I mean. I don't follow that at all.

Her response was essentially the same for apartheid:

> That's another I don't really follow either because these are like current events to do with politics, and I think we shouldn't even concern ourselves with them as much . . . See I've heard about South Africa, but that's in like the presidential thing, you know what I mean? I just tune out. I have two kids and when that stuff comes on the news, I just go and feed the kids or call someone on the phone for a couple of minutes. I don't keep up with things like that. Medical things, and you know, like kidnapping and drugs, I know a lot about that stuff.

In what appears to be a judgment central to the learning process, subjects tended to rate the salient issues—drug abuse and AIDS—as "easy to understand." These results suggest that people find that issues they learn about exclusively in the media (such as foreign news or policies being made in Washington) are more difficult to comprehend than issues that they can experience, no matter how distantly, in their own lives.

If television were more successful in communicating about South Africa and SDI, and less successful on drug abuse and AIDS, it seems that learning effectiveness has less to do with how issues "play" in the medium, and a great deal to do with how the audience feels about the issues. The abstract, distant, or more difficult issues seem to be more daunting in print than they are on television. Characteristics that attract and maintain the attention of the audience (TV factors) are correlated with learning about *low* salience issues (such as South Africa and SDI), while the expository and contextual factors in print media increase learning about *high* salience issues (drug abuse and AIDS).

Our audience evaluators provide considerable support for this thesis (see table 5.2). The audience judged television more "attention grabbing" overall than magazines or newspapers. In our experiments, a medium's attention-grabbing quotient translated into more learning in stories that were low in salience—apartheid in South Africa, Star Wars—or high in difficulty—the stock market crash. A similar effect was apparent for pictures and graphics. Television was, of course, rated highest on all visual effects, but visuals alone did not predict learning for all kinds of stories. Visuals were only important in those stories for which the experimental subjects initially exhibited low levels of interest, South Africa and SDI, for example, and for which the visuals provided an explanatory narrative for the story independent of the audio explanation (Crigler, Just, and Neuman, 1991). In the case of South Africa, the visuals told the story of black rioting in Johannesberg, while the Star Wars animated graphic showed just how the space weapons were supposed to work. These visual explanations helped to make difficult and distant issues accessible to the audience.

Now if breaking the attention barrier and making news stories accessible are the keys to learning about issues in which the mass public has little interest, what does it take to enhance learning about issues in which people are interested? In the AIDS experiment, subjects in both print conditions learned more than those exposed to TV. This was the kind of issue where the audience evaluators rated the magazine and newspaper stories as more factual and contextualizing than the television stories. Magazine coverage, in particular, was seen as conveying facts, economic analysis, description of effects, and information about what people could do about the problem. Since AIDS was a

Table 5.2 Audience Evaluations by Issue by Medium (Means from 7-Point Scales)

	S. Africa			SDI			Crash			Drugs			AIDS		
	TV	Newsp.	Mag.	TV	Newsp.	Mag.	TV	Newsp.	Mag.	TV	Newsp.	Mag.	TV	Newsp.	Mag.
Involving:															
Att'n. grabbing	5.3	4.0	4.4*	5.4	5.0	4.5	3.7	3.8	4.5	6.5	5.5	5.7	5.7	4.2	4.8*
Emotional	5.3	4.3	4.4	4.9	4.9	4.0	3.2	3.0	3.7	5.9	4.5	5.5	4.9	3.9	4.5
Surprising	5.1	3.1	3.6**	4.5	3.1	3.7*	4.0	3.2	4.5*	4.9	4.5	4.3	4.7	3.0	3.5**
Human interest	6.1	4.9	5.3*	5.5	5.7	4.8	4.6	3.9	4.8	6.8	6.5	6.3	6.0	5.9	5.8
Pictures	6.2	1.3	2.2**	6.3	3.7	3.9**	4.3	2.8	3.1*	6.4	3.6	3.3**	5.9	1.7	2.2**
Contextualizing:															
Politics	4.7	3.8	4.4	4.5	5.1	4.0	3.0	4.1	4.5	2.4	2.9	4.0	4.1	4.4	4.6
History	2.6	3.8	3.1	3.4	3.1	3.3	3.2	3.6	4.4	3.0	4.3	5.2**	3.3	3.3	4.6
Economics	2.1	3.0	2.4	3.0	4.6	4.0	4.8	5.3	4.9	3.7	4.8	5.2	4.2	4.4	5.1
Causes	4.0	5.1	3.9	3.6	3.9	3.2	3.8	4.3	4.7	5.3	5.7	5.9	4.6	5.2	5.4
Effects	4.2	4.6	3.4	4.3	4.4	3.5	4.9	4.0	5.1*	6.1	6.5	6.0	5.3	5.4	5.9
People can do	2.0	1.8	2.3	2.3	1.7	2.4	3.0	2.1	3.5	1.6	3.3	3.4**	3.1	4.1	4.7*
Facts	4.5	5.2	4.5	4.8	5.0	4.4	4.3	4.8	5.0	5.5	6.3	5.5	4.7	5.5	6.0

**F significant at .01.
*F significant at .05.

story (like drug abuse) in which people were already interested, it is not surprising that attention-getting was not a critical variable for learning. Furthermore, in the AIDS experiment, subjects were comparatively well-informed about the basic facts of the disease so that most of the learning that took place in the experiment centered on implications, predictions, and policies. As the objective presentational analysis indicated, it was precisely in these contextual aspects that magazines excelled.

The stock market experiment represents a special case. The subjects in the learning experiments reported a fair degree of interest in the economy but low levels of attention to economic news. Most people thought this issue was particularly difficult to understand. As one woman remarked during an in-depth interview, "I don't really understand about the market—not even to explain it." In the experiment, no media group significantly outperformed the others on the issue of the stock market crash. The pattern, however, showed that subjects in the magazine condition learned relatively more than subjects in other conditions. Interestingly, on the topic of the stock market crash, audience evaluators rated magazine news, rather than television news, as the most attention-grabbing, most dramatic, and most "people-oriented" presentation of the news.

The combination of the media experiments and the audience evaluational analysis by issue supports the constructionist hypothesis that the nature of the issue is critical to a medium's effectiveness as a learning environment. For issues in which salience is high, the analytic context can increase learning, but where salience is low an effective medium has to break the attention barrier.

Testing the Attention-Barrier Hypothesis

As an explicit test of the attention-barrier hypothesis, we separated out our subjects on the basis of their level of interest in each news topic. We would expect that the effectiveness of television in breaking the attention barrier would be most apparent among people who are not so interested in particular issues. Figure 5.5 shows the media learning patterns separately for both low- and high-interest subjects.

Here the media differences stand out. Television is distinctly more effective for the low-interest respondents, and magazines provided a context almost as hospitable. The success of television in com-

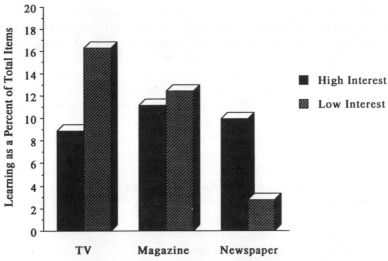

Figure 5.5   Issue Knowledge Gain by Medium by Interest

municating information might be explained by the visual excitement that broke the attention barrier; the strength of magazines more likely lies in the characteristic style of newsmagazine writing, which provides an analytical context for new information. Both the presentational and evaluative analyses of news coverage in Chapter 3 showed that contextualization (i.e., providing definitions, causes, and consequences for issues) was far more common in newsmagazines than in any other medium. In the experiments, it seems, the medium that provided either visual excitement (TV) *or* verbal context (newsmagazines) drew people into the story and compensated for low initial interest in some issues. Our experiments suggest that television's exciting, involving qualities and explanatory visuals break the attention barrier and make the personal relevance of an issue apparent. People with low initial interest, or who worry that the issue is too difficult to understand, can be drawn into a television story.

Print media, on the other hand, are more factual and complete, and when the interest already exists, are a particularly efficient medium for information retrieval, but only when the citizen is motivated to do the retrieving. So for an issue like AIDS, for which the vast majority of our respondents already had high interest and knowledge, the attention grabbing was unnecessary, while background information was valued by the audience.

Complementary Media

Our research on the interaction of media coverage and issue characteristics in the mass audience demonstrates that broadcast and print media can be and, in practice, often are complementary. It is simply not true that the vast majority of American citizens use either print or broadcast media exclusively and avoid information from any other source. Although people are willing, in response to the insistence of the survey interviewer, to identify a primary or preferred source of news, the evidence is that only about 10 percent of the population depends exclusively on TV news and half regularly follow both television and newspaper news. In addition, the evidence of our in-depth interviews is that most people pick up ideas and information from a wide mix of news media, entertainment media, and personal conversations. If television is particularly successful at breaking the attention barrier and getting people interested, and print media are particularly successful at providing the in-depth follow-up, then the relationship is synergistic rather than antagonistic. It might be that the political communications process would be enhanced by a more self-conscious coordination between print and broadcast media.

One disappointing note in our research on media differences, however, is that the professional journalists themselves have very little feedback on how well the information they present to the public is "getting through" (Kiolbassa, 1989). When first asked what people learned from their stories, they responded with variations on a theme of "how would I know?"

Political Communication: A One-Way Street?

Figure 1.1 illustrates an idealized model of the interacting elements of the constructionist model of political communication: public issues, mass media, and the citizenry. Two-headed arrows connect each element to illustrate the simultaneity and interaction of meaning construction as new events occur and are interpreted by reporters and citizens. Citizens talk with each other and rely on other nonmedia sources for information about issues. Reporters talk with each other and interact closely with the central actors on the political stage.

Citizens hear a great deal of what the reporters think and how they frame events. But what do reporters know of the perspectives of the public at large?

Drawing on Kiolbassa's extensive interviews with eighteen of the journalists who wrote the stories on SDI, AIDS, and drug abuse used in the experimental research (1989), we looked closely at what they knew about public perceptions of their work, and what they felt they ought to know. One newspaper reporter responds: "Geez, I wish I knew [how the audience reacted]. It's awfully hard to figure out . . . what impact you're having on public thinking . . . What I'd hope is, not to create, but, increase a sense of concern about AIDS." Although virtually all of the journalists interviewed explained that they had no systematic or reliable way to assess how the public was responding and what it was learning from what they wrote, some seemed to think that was as it ought to be. A magazine journalist writing on SDI explains:

> I don't know if it's influenced them at all. I have no idea . . .
> There are [letters to the editor], but I don't think *Time* generates that many letters on a story like this [SDI]. Those tend to be generated by cover stories . . . I have no idea. *We're properly insulated. We don't want to be worried about what people think. We have a separate department that worries about that.*

A *Globe* reporter was more circumspect:

> The editors try to make the story more compelling, and the feedback they give you . . . goes into making it a better story when it's in the paper . . . As I recall, I got pretty decent feedback . . . from editors, and maybe from some readers. But that doesn't do much for me in terms of giving me a feel of whether the story worked . . . In the absence of knowing what readers think, it's nice to know that editors who pay your salary liked what you did.

Our observation about what might be characterized as an institutionalized insensitivity to public reactions (other than to crude measurements of circulation and Nielsen ratings) is not new (Gans, 1979; Robinson and Levy, 1986). But it represents an area of special promise for further inquiry. Many reporters are curious about public reactions.

Journalists' notions of which media are most successful at political communication are contradicted by our data. There would appear to be ample room to extend and strengthen the political communications process by fine-tuning journalistic traditions to take advantage more appropriately of complementary media strengths.

SIX
Learning from the News

As we explained at the outset, there is a considerable literature that puts most of the responsibility for informing citizens on the citizens themselves. Researchers in the "uninformed voter" tradition tend to blame people for being too self-involved and uninterested in the polity, or for lacking the capacity to become informed. Our depth interviews demonstrate that regardless of the amount of factual information people can recall on demand, they are capable of constructing richly human conceptualizations of public issues from their personal and mediated experiences. In the previous chapters, we showed how different journalistic styles of presentation characteristic of different media affect the accessibility of information.[1] We turn now to the role of individual citizens in acquiring knowledge about public affairs. We are interested here in what it takes to become informed—how much attention to which media, and how sophisticated people have to be to understand and learn about the complex issues that confront democratic citizens in today's world. Finally we reassess how successful different media are in communicating with people who have varying levels of interest and sophistication in politics.

Individual Differences in Media Learning

Media researchers have repeatedly found that "general knowledge and skills for abstract inference" are highly correlated with learning from news (Collins, 1982; Hoijer, 1984). While knowledge and inferential ability can both be considered evidence of sophistication, the two factors distinguish people from one another in very different ways. Inferential ability applies across topics, that is, people have more or less ability to infer or analogize; whereas knowledge is specific, arising from an individual's idiosyncratic tastes or interests in various topics.

A number of researchers hold the view that learning about politics is essentially an attribute "determined by a single underlying structure" (Schroder, Driver, and Streufert, 1967; Neuman, 1986; Rosenberg, 1988). Less skilled individuals may find new information overwhelming (Andriate and Beatty, 1988) and will have a hard time learning, regardless of their interest in the topic.

Even if cognitive ability makes it easier to integrate new information in general, the amount of knowledge one has acquired on a specific subject provides cognitive support for learning, regardless of ability level (Fiske, Kinder, and Larter, 1983). People who know something about a topic have to make less of an effort to find a home for new bits of data than individuals who have to start from scratch.

Looking at the responses to the questionnaires filled out by our experimental subjects, we found that their cognitive skill, their interest in the issues, and their attention to news on the subject all had an impact on what they knew about issues to begin with. Table 6.1 shows the results of a multiple regression equation on the information indices *before* the experiments. The regression indicates that both cognitive skill and interest in an issue contribute significantly to a higher level of information, but paying attention to news about the topic is essential to acquiring knowledge, independent of interest or cognitive skill.

Table 6.1   Individual Attributes: Regression on Prior Issue Knowledge

Individual Attribute	B	Beta	Significance
Attention to issue news	.59	.35	.001
Cognitive skill	.14	.28	.001
Education	.28	.11	.003
Issue important	.20	.11	.003
Personal efficacy	.01	.01	.647
Political efficacy	.02	.04	.261
Print prime news source	.18	.03	.392
(Constant)	5.00	—	.000
Multiple R	.51	—	—
R Square	.26	—	—

The Problem with Television

Given the extensive literature that charts the decline of participation in American politics since the advent of television, we might expect that where our subjects got their news would have an important impact on what they knew about the issues. Most of the anti-television literature is based on data which show lower levels of information among people who rely on television news rather than newspapers or magazines (Chaffee, Ward, and Tipton, 1970; Patterson, 1980; Robinson and Levy, 1986). Our results do not dispute those findings. Subjects who claimed to rely on magazines or newspapers as their primary source of news scored an average of one point higher (8.06) on the pre-exposure information index than those who relied on TV (who averaged 6.95). The results give aid and comfort to the school of communications researchers who blame television's visual emphasis in story selection and its exceedingly dense and brief coverage of topics for declining levels of political information (Epstein, 1973; Robinson, 1976; Robinson and Sheehan, 1983).

When we look at who the readers and viewers are, however, we find that what is really causing the television-is-the-problem effect is the preference of people with lower cognitive skills to get their news from television. Three-quarters of the least cognitively skilled prefer broad-

Table 6.2   Preferred Source of News, Prior Knowledge, and Cognitive Skill

| | Preferred News Source | | |
	TV	Radio	Newspaper/ Magazine
Low cognitive skill:			
Prior knowledge score:			
Mean	6.1	7.1	6.7
Percent	58	09	21
(N)	(272)	(40)	(100)
High cognitive skill:			
Prior knowledge score:			
Mean	8.3	9.1	8.8
Percent	42	12	46
(N)	(175)	(49)	(189)

Note: F for 2-way interaction: .028 (not significant).

cast news, while just over half of the most skilled prefer either news-papers or newsmagazines (significant at $p < .05$). The entire relationship between knowledge of the issues and media surveillance habits washes out when we control for cognitive skill (see table 6.2). Because the experimental design enabled us to include a cognitive skills test, we are able to show that the relationship between reading a newspaper and knowing a lot about public affairs is spurious. Those who are more skilled know more, regardless of whether they read newspapers or watch TV. Table 6.2 shows no statistically significant difference in the average level of knowledge of either high- or low-skilled individuals in terms of their media preferences. Those with low skills scored about 6.5 on the prior knowledge index and those with high skills scored about 8.5. When survey researchers conclude that television depresses news learning, they are confounding the effects of cognitive skill with media habits.

Learning: The Linear Effect

Turning from knowledge to learning, we can ask just how much cognitive skill, education, or attention to news did people need to learn something about a topic? Is there some important qualifying threshold that individuals must cross in order to become politically informed? Figures 6.1–6.3 show that scores on the index of prior knowledge improve linearly by at least one right answer on the information index for each level of education, cognitive skill, or attention to issues. For example, individuals who did not complete high school scored on average less than 5 correct answers on the prior knowledge index, while those who completed high school scored 6 and college graduates scored 7.

When we looked at information gained in the experiments, the same linear pattern appeared. At least in the short term, no matter what the subject's level of education, cognitive skill, or previous attention to the issue, there is a measurable gain in information about the issues. In each experiment, the amount learned by individuals in each cognitive or attention category brought them at or above the initial level of knowledge of those at the next highest cognitive or attention level (see figs. 6.1–6.3). After a 6-minute news exposure, for example, the high school graduate averaged the same number of right answers as the college graduate did before the experiment began.

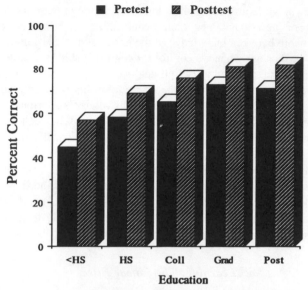

Figure 6.1   Issue Knowledge Gain by Level of Education

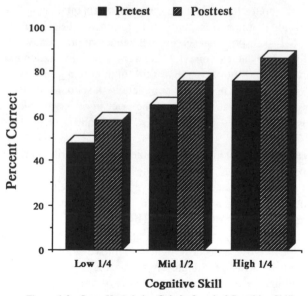

Figure 6.2   Issue Knowledge Gain by Level of Cognitive Skill

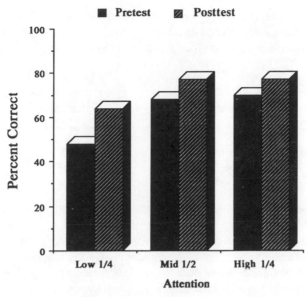

Figure 6.3   Issue Knowledge Gain by Level of Issue Attention

The results are slightly different for attention than for other variables. A high level of attention to news neither improved knowledge nor learning scores. It seems that only an "average" amount of interest in political issues is sufficient to provide a solid base for further learning. The results suggest that knowledge leads to learning, just as learning leads to knowledge in a "spiraling process." As Hoijer notes, the process of comprehending news is "an act of remembering with the implicit question: What does this mean in relation to what I already know?" (Hoijer, 1984).

Compensatory Advantages in Learning

The literature reinforces the view that people who have some information about a topic are at a great advantage when it comes to learning more (Tichenor, Donohue, and Olien, 1970; Robinson, 1972). We were so impressed with the learning advantage of people who already had a great deal of information about a topic that we decided to see whether paying attention to the news could compensate for a deficit in cognitive skill. To answer that question we divided the subjects into four groups depending on whether they scored above or below the median on cognitive skill and on attention to news about the issue in the experiment. The resulting four groups were as follows:

Group 1	*Group 2*
low cognitive skill	low cognitive skill
low attention	high attention
Group 3	*Group 4*
high cognitive skill	high cognitive skill
low attention	high attention

We expected that those subjects who had deficits in both cognitive skill and attention to news (group 1) would score the fewest correct responses on the information index, while those who were strong in both skill and attentiveness (group 4) would score the highest; but for those groups that were deficient only in either motivation or cognitive skill (group 2 or group 3), it was an open question. We thought it likely that the ability of individuals to overcome a deficit in either cognitive skill, or for that matter in education, might vary with the complexity of the material that would have to be mastered. Therefore, we analyzed the results by issue (see figs. 6.4–6.8).

Analysis of variance indicates that the differences among the four groups, group 1 to group 4, are significant for every issue we investigated. This was no surprise. We expected that subjects who were disadvantaged with respect to cognitive skill and who paid less than average attention to news would know and learn less than those who had the advantages of both cognitive skill and attention. Figures 6.4–6.8 show, however, that the importance of both cognitive skill and attention to news vary considerably by issue. Subjects in group 1 (those who had lower cognitive skills and were not motivated to follow the news) were at the greatest disadvantage in those issues where media are the primary or sole sources of information—foreign affairs, defense policy, and the stock market. On those issues, group 1 scored on average about 5 correct answers, only half the score of group 4 (high cognitive skill and high attention to news). By way of contrast, for the issues of drug abuse and AIDS, where other people and the entertainment media are significant sources of issue information, there were relatively small differences among all four cognitive skill and attention groups.

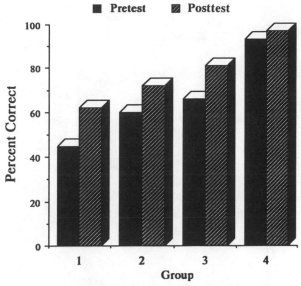

Figure 6.4   The Compensatory Effect: The Interaction of Interest
and Cognitive Skill—South Africa

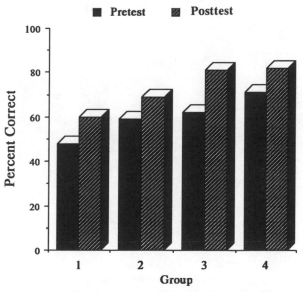

Figure 6.5   The Compensatory Effect: The Interaction of Interest
and Cognitive Skill—SDI

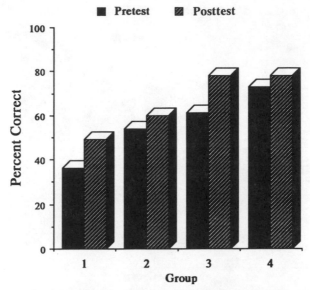

Figure 6.6　The Compensatory Effect: The Interaction of Interest
and Cognitive Skill—Crash

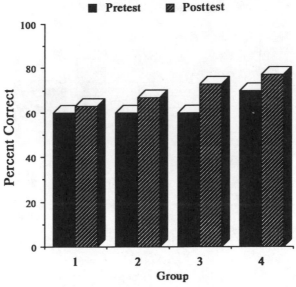

Figure 6.7　The Compensatory Effect: The Interaction of Interest
and Cognitive Skill—Drug Abuse

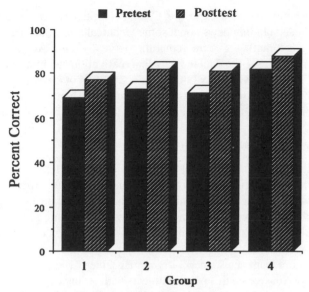

Figure 6.8   The Compensatory Effect: The Interaction of Interest
and Cognitive Skill—AIDS

An important democratic concern is explored by comparing groups 2 and 3. Can simply paying attention to news compensate for a lack of cognitive skill? We noted that on the prior knowledge index, the difference in mean scores between subjects in group 2 (low cognitive skill/high interest) and group 3 (high cognitive skill/low interest) was less than one item. Separate pre-exposure T-tests for each issue in the experiments indicate that the difference between the scores of groups 2 and 3 is *not* statistically significant. As far as the topics we looked at were concerned, virtually anyone who was interested enough to follow the news had as much information to start with as someone who was cognitively skilled but not particularly interested in the topic.

After exposure to news, all of the groups showed an increase on the issue information scales, and in most instances the learning pattern for all four groups paralleled the pattern for prior knowledge: the information gains for groups 2 and 3 were not significantly different. On the two issues, however, that involved technical information—Star Wars and the stock market crash—subjects with high cognitive skills and low attention learned significantly more than those with low cognitive skill and high attention, even though the two groups had scored about the same before the news exposure. Clearly cognitive skill is an advantage in understanding news about some technical topics, such as SDI and the stock market. For the remaining issues—South Africa, drug abuse, and AIDS—the data indicate that motivation can indeed compensate for cognitive ability both in the acquisition of knowledge (assessed in the pre-exposure information scale) and in learning (assessed by the difference between pre- and post-exposure information scales).

Media Deficits and Compensations

If cognitive skill is not essential to learning about most topics, it could still be important to learning from different media. Our experiments provided an important opportunity to test the reputed appeal of television to the "lowest common denominator" versus the "high brow" advantage of newspapers and magazines. Would people with low cognitive skills learn more from television while the highly skilled learned more from newspapers or newsmagazines? The data were extremely persuasive on this point. Subjects with strong cognitive skills showed no special learning gain in the print media, as opposed to television. They got the same amount of information out of both. Nor did subjects with low cognitive skill score much better in the TV condition than in magazines; they found that all of the media posed difficulties. But the average subject found it far more difficult to learn in the newspaper condition than from television or from newsmagazines (see fig. 6.9). In the newspaper condition, subjects with average cognitive skills (who scored in either quartile around the median in the cognitive skills test) learned less than average in the experiments. This was not true for either of the other two media conditions. The results indicate that the structure and style of newspaper journalism make it harder for people with just average cognitive skills to learn information about political issues. The presentation of news on television and in magazines, however, seems to enhance the ability of ordinary people to learn, so much so that their performance is not significantly different from people with above-average cognitive skills.

Interaction Effects: Medium, Issue, and Citizen

Our evidence supports a constructionist view of learning, one that depends on the qualities that individuals in the audience bring to particular topics in the news media. People with strong cognitive skills or

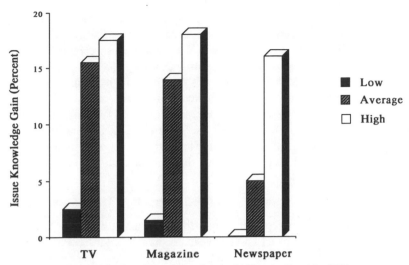

Figure 6.9   Issue Knowledge Gain by Medium by Cognitive Skill

more education, for example, were more likely to recognize the importance of foreign and technical issues and to follow those issues in the news. As a result, cognitively skilled individuals were likely to benefit from two learning advantages: ability and motivation.

We are able to show, however, that it is not particularly consequential which medium people depend on for news. The apparent superiority of print news sources is merely a reflection of the media preferences of more cognitively skilled individuals.

As far as learning is concerned, we were not surprised to find that cognitively skilled individuals learned the most, and in television as well as print. Even those cognitively skilled individuals who had not been attentive to news about South Africa and Star Wars had a significant edge in learning. We found, however, that the advantage conferred by cognitive skill varied with the issue. Individuals with strong cognitive skills did not learn appreciably more than those who were less skilled about an issue like drug abuse, which is characterized by a high degree of public interest and knowledge. In fact, for both health issues, drug abuse and AIDS, even the combined disadvantage of low cognitive skill and low attention to news did not result in a significant deficit in either knowledge or learning.

The results also show that while cognitive ability is an advantage, motivation can compensate with respect to most, nontechnical, public issues. In all of the experiments except Star Wars and the stock market crash, there were no differences in the amount learned by the cognitively skilled versus the high attention group.

The interaction of the media with cognitive ability reinforces the general conclusion about media-linked journalistic formats. The evidence shows that newspapers were particularly disadvantageous to people with average cognitive skills. Since magazines are as literacy based as newspapers, the reason for magazine superiority must lie in its style of news presentation, rather than the modality of print.

A Downsian Model of Political Information Management

We know from our depth interviews that citizens are busy people and those who wish to be informed have to do so in the interstices of many other life activities. As Downs argues, people try to acquire information at the smallest cost, that is, with the least effort (Downs, 1957). Rational choice theory counsels us that the cost of a piece of information should be viewed against its prospective benefits. The media may design news stories to cut information costs either by identifying valuable information in the story or by attracting the audience's attention along some other dimension. Applying the "uses and gratifications" approach to the design of news suggests that entertaining stories have a higher benefit to cost ratio than dry and dull stories. The cost of a particular story may vary, therefore, depending on the way particular news items are presented in the media. Chapter 5 shows that television, in particular, can lower information costs for stories that seem distant and personally irrelevant.

Information costs are not only affected on the media side but on the individual side of the equation as well. Some individuals may store and retrieve information more efficiently than others. One could argue that individuals who are skilled at storing and retrieving information or people who have already acquired knowledge about a particular topic have lower costs for integrating new information than people who are less skilled or less interested.

Woodall, Davis, and Sahin (1983) propose an explanation for the phenomenon that people who know about an issue have a learning advantage over those who are less knowledgeable. They describe two kinds of processing: top-down and bottom-up. In the top-down process, people who are knowledgeable about a particular topic are able to scan the data efficiently to find new information; in the bottom-up process, however, those who are unknowledgeable are forced to rely on the information package itself to construct meaning from the information. Donohew, Tipton, and Haney (1978) offer some empirical support for Woodall et al.'s theory. They report that individuals with high prior knowledge appear to pursue efficient, "narrow-focused" strategies for obtaining relevant information, while less knowledgeable people employ less efficient, broad-focused strategies. If knowledgeable and unknowledgeable people pursue different strategies for learning, then the learning efficiency of a news medium will depend on how hospitable it is to the particular strategy the individual is pursuing.

The evidence from our experiments is that the more accommodating media, television and magazines, offered their audiences some contextual information that was lacking in the newspaper presentation. In the case of television, context was achieved primarily through exciting and reinforcing visuals (or animated graphics); in the case of magazines, the context was found in its more discursive presentation which made room for a number of analytic hooks, such as historical background and economic impact. We can presume that either form of contextualization cuts the cost of storing and retrieving information. The media learning differences that we found in our data point to some recommendations that all of the news media can adopt to cut the information costs for people who are not highly skilled or very knowledgeable about a topic. For example, our audience evaluators found television to be particularly effective in making abstract issues more comprehensible. Some of television's visual images and attention-attracting devices, however, could be adapted by print media. Likewise, television and newspapers could provide the informational context that make magazines so effective for learning.

The main hazard of providing context is that it is almost impossible to accomplish within the strictly neutral norms of television and newspaper journalism. Still, it may be worth finding where the boundaries lie between maximal context and minimum bias. The data here suggest that contextualizing the news could compensate members of the public who have to overcome deficits in cognitive skill or motivation to become informed about complex issues.

SEVEN
Constructing Meaning

Our research focuses on that delicate connection between private life and public responsibility that is the charge of democracy. How is it that some matters become common knowledge, the taken-for-granted components of a nation's collective memory, while others are only dimly perceived, if at all, by the public at large? Our attention is drawn to the mass media, through which individuals forge the link between public and private life.

The constructionist model of political communication on which we have drawn in this study triangulates media, audience, and issue domains. Theory in this tradition focuses on the conditions of effective mass communication. The communication outcome, be it learning, persuasion, resonance, or interest, depends on the character of the communications source (including complex norms of professional journalism and the nature of the news medium itself), the character of the audience (diversely skilled and interested in public affairs), as well as the nature of the public issues in question. This approach emphasizes that the growth of common knowledge is gradual, iterative, and interpretive. The central problematics of this research paradigm focus on the connections made, and the connections missed, between the citizens' interests and understandings and the language of public discourse in the news media.

The Active Audience
Media Agendas and Audience Agendas

One of the critical findings of this study is the disjuncture between what the mass media emphasize and what the media audience tells us is important and relevant to their lives. Comparing the depth interviews and experimental results with the media content analyses, we see very different priorities. The media agenda, governed by periodic reporting, is preoccupied with the specifics of the day's or week's events, especially the activities of public officials (Sigal, 1973; Tuchman, 1978; Gans, 1979; Hess, 1981). In contrast, the public's interest in the daily workings of government and foreign affairs is mitigated by pressing personal and immediate concerns. People express less concern about Congressional votes on specific weapon systems than they do about the larger issues of war and peace. They may be a bit hazy about the details of a National Academy of Science report on AIDS but care deeply about a range of health and safety issues in their communities.

The disjuncture between the popular and media framing of public issues casts some doubt on the overly convenient refrain of the agenda-setting tradition to the effect that if the media cannot tell people what to think, the media can demonstrably tell them what to think about (Cohen, 1963; McCombs and Shaw, 1972). Extensive news coverage of apartheid in South Africa, for example, which was especially prominent on television, was not mirrored in public concern. At the same time, the public's deep concern about drug abuse and related crime problems was only weakly reflected in media coverage.

Our interviews suggest that at least part of the public's limited interest in the official side of national and international affairs results from a profound sense of powerlessness. Ironically, the cosmopolitan and investigative style of what is usually defined as journalism at its best may reinforce this sense of powerlessness through an emphasis on irony, often evident in the summary line of a television report, or by building the story line around the hopeless complexity of issues. Our subjects reacted with special enthusiasm to information about how to take control of public issues. We found, for example, that a fairly technical magazine story about the stock market was given high marks for interest by our audience judges because it emphasized "what you can do about the problem." As the norms of journalistic practice evolve in time, we think it would be useful for journalists to experiment more with incorporating the dimension of civic action into the substance of the news story.

Our depth interviews illustrate how the audience actively frames and interprets a variety of public issues reported in the news media. In reading through the transcripts, one is struck by the sheer diversity of interpretation. Virtually all of our interviewees freely mix together exemplary events and ideas drawn from their own life experiences, books, motion pictures, and entertainment television as well as the traditional news media as they explain their thinking on political topics. When the issues of drug abuse and crime arise, people draw on their own or a friend's or relative's experience with a recent robbery or draw on their professional experience with crime as a store clerk or teacher. People pick up a variety of statistics and impressions about trends (most often, of course, that things are getting worse) and intermingle the numbers with the narratives. When dealing with distant events like race relations in South Africa, they draw heavily on what they know of race relations in the United States. Their experiences and impressions, naturally, are very different, and each element in the mix adds an interpretive flavor to their understanding of what makes an issue important.

We demonstrated that journalistic norms tend to result in the use of quite similar conceptual frames for the issues we examined in television, magazine, and newspaper coverage. Regardless of the medium in which they work, journalists eschew the moral frame which figures prominently in the public's understanding of issues. The public, in contrast, relished and drew out the moral dimension in the human impact of issues, and underscored the moral dimensions of public policies. The moral emphasis was not limited to the more personalized issues of drug abuse and AIDS but arose frequently, even in discussions of Star Wars, with personal anecdotes about the need to exhibit strength to avoid unnecessary conflict, and in apartheid with an emphasis, sometimes religious in character, on the need to uphold the dignity of all persons.

These findings resonate with the findings of Lane (1962), Graber (1988), and most recently Gamson (1992), who note the striking disjunctures between the morselized and personalized language of private thought and discussion and the official and public discourse that dominates the language of journalists and politicians. The disjuncture in conceptualization also underscores the disconfirmation of the agenda-setting hypothesis. People think for themselves, and media and official versions of problems and events make up only part of their schema for public issues.

The disjuncture in public and media frames demonstrates that alternative frames are out there in the public discourse on issues. In general, the journalists have shied away from the moral dimension, remaining on the relatively safe ground of objectified news (Schudson, 1978;

Hallin, 1985; Dennis, 1989). Since some of these moral frames reinforce parochial and even bigoted values, it is not clear that the media's cautious avoidance of such perspectives serves best to enhance
democratic competence. Rather than hoping that news frames will
overwhelm popular conceptions, the media could confront those conceptualizations head on and provide a range of challenging, alternative views, or as Gans termed it, a multiperspectival approach to
public issues.

Mediated Learning

Our survey of more than 1,500 experimental subjects found, as do
other researchers, that people who prefer to get their news from television were, on the whole, less knowledgeable than those who preferred
print news. Because our experimental pretest not only included an assessment of prior knowledge of each issue but also a brief cognitive
skills test, we were able to show that the entire relationship between
television news preference and lower knowledge scores is spurious.
The TV–low knowledge correlation was entirely accounted for by the
cognitive skill differential between those who prefer television as a
news source and those who prefer newspapers or magazines. It appears that television news coverage has been blamed for the skewed
media preferences of the cognitively advantaged.[1]

Had we ended our analysis of news learning with assessments of
knowledge and media surveillance habits, we might have concluded
that there are no media effects—that all of the presumed effects of media are nothing more than the reflection of real differences among individuals. The intense examination of a fragment of the learning process
that we achieved in our experiments, however, shows that the impact
of media style on learning is actually a complex interaction between
the journalist's presentation and the individual's psychological
ground.

The key finding of the learning experiments is that television was
more successful in communicating information about topics that were
of low salience to the audience, while print media were superior in
conveying information about topics that had high salience. Furthermore, our audience-judges were able to identify for us just what it was
about particular stories that made them more successful in the learning
process. Television, they said, grabbed their attention, surprised

them, and gave the stories more human interest. They credited television with being significantly more interesting than other media in reporting about South Africa and Star Wars. On the other hand, the audience-judges found that both newspapers and newsmagazines were particularly helpful in describing the history and explaining what people could do about the problems of drug abuse and AIDS—issues for which the print media were effective in the learning experiments.

The correlation of our content analyses with our experimental findings support a media complementarity hypothesis. Both print and television news styles can optimize learning, but for different issues. It might be tempting to argue that stories that television excelled in reporting involved foreign affairs or technical information, or that print media enhance learning for less mediated issues, but we have only one data point on each and cannot make such fine distinctions. Testing more refined hypotheses about television versus print issues would require learning experiments on a number of topics.

What we can say with somewhat more confidence is that topics that appear to be more effective in print than on television appear to be identified by the subjective interest and, therefore, the knowledge base of the audience on that issue. Television can break the attention barrier for issues of low salience and may reinforce new learning through coordinated visual information. The experiments in which visuals carried a significant amount of narrative information—South Africa and Star Wars—were the ones in which television learning was greatest (Crigler, Just, and Neuman, 1991). Newspapers and magazines are better sources for new information when the audience is already motivated to pay attention to the story and is seeking the kind of contextual richness in which the print media excel.

Individual Differences

Whatever the media had to offer by way of arousing interest or presenting information made little difference, we found, to those individuals who were cognitively skilled or already interested in the topic. Subjects advantaged on either the skill or interest dimension were better informed than those who were less advantaged. On two of the five topics, cognitively skilled individuals learned more than those who had been attentive to news about the topic in the past, and these issues tended to be technical (Star Wars and the stock market). On the remaining issues, there was no statistical difference in the issue knowledge gain between those who were skilled but not so attentive and those who were attentive but not so skilled. We conclude, therefore, that paying attention to the news, whether in newspapers or on television, can compensate for deficiencies in cognitive skill.

We must offer one caveat, however. Our experiments in learning revealed that subjects with average cognitive skill performed most poorly in the newspaper condition, significantly worse than those in the newsmagazine condition. It seems inescapable to conclude that people with average skills may not be best served by the current structure of newspaper news. In expressing a preference for television news, people may be making an effective learning choice, but the experiments show that television is not the only alternative. In our study, results for magazines indicate that when average people were "on task" they learned almost as much from magazines as from television. Clearly, the problem does not lie with print. It may be that if some of the presentational devices of magazines were adopted by newspapers, people might feel more comfortable using newspaper news. The success of *USA Today* gives some support to the view that new styles of newspaper journalism can find a niche in the news media market. *USA Today*, while it offers full color visuals, makes little attempt to offer the analysis or contextual richness of newsmagazines. The success of a variety of television newsmagazine programs suggests the same approach might be effective on TV. It would be interesting to see whether the adoption of the contextual richness of a magazine style might not be an appealing as well as enriching format for both newspapers and television.

The overall finding of our experiments is that people do learn from their media encounters—perhaps not a lot each time, but the result of a habit of news attention is an accumulation of political information. We conclude that it is less important how people want to get their news than *whether* they want to get news. As a result, all of the news media—print as well as broadcasting—bear the democratic burden of making news about public affairs accessible and inviting to the audience.

Issue Salience

In our discussions, we have emphasized the importance of the issue domain for political communication. We have demonstrated that issue salience is critical to understanding the dynamics of political learning and even to the effectiveness of different journalistic styles of communication. People, naturally (and perhaps necessarily), do not have an equal level of interest in every topic. Nor do all people have similar interests. But the individual's interest, information, and affect related to any issue have important consequences for the way that messages communicated through the media are appreciated by the audience.

Analysis of the coverage of five issues demonstrated that the overall pattern of news coverage was similar across media. Television, newspapers, and newsmagazines gave roughly the same proportion of attention to national and international issues, and to the more technically oriented and human interest stories we studied. These similarities support the view that news selection and framing is governed in the first place by professional norms and external reality (Gans, 1979).

This, however, was not the end of the story. We also found significant disparities in coverage that apparently arise from what might be called the mission of the medium. Newspapers, for example, have a unique view of their role in social registry (deaths and marriages) and in the archiving of economic data. Among the issues we studied, the stock market was more thoroughly covered in the business pages of newspapers and the national and international sections of newsmagazines than on television, while at least one story with exciting visual footage (South Africa) was given much greater coverage on television than in newspapers or magazines.

The differences in media coverage of particular issues is predictable on some dimensions but not on others. For example, the fact that the stock market is routinely and extensively reported in newspapers means that individuals can plan a media surveillance strategy around that difference in media coverage. But it is a lot harder to tell which stories *are* visual or *when* a story is going to be visual and when not. Consider coverage of apartheid in South Africa. The story was lavishly covered on television right before our experiments in 1986, but shortly thereafter, the South African government banned television cameras. When the cameras were forced out, the amount of television news about South Africa plummeted. Clearly the news value of the South Africa story did not change because of the camera ban, but television coverage was dramatically affected. These differences mean that neither the public nor communications researchers can take uniform news values for granted. Individuals should (and most do) use a mix of news media if they want to capture stories that could be downgraded by the constraints (news hole, visuals) of a particular medium. Researchers would also benefit from an appreciation of the complementarity of media usage and coverage, and should not rely on a single medium to provide a picture of news coverage. It is important to emphasize that the differences we observed are not the exclusive problem of television, nor is the television emphasis on visuals essentially trivializing. The South African example shows that visual emphasis can actually lead to proportionately greater coverage of an issue on TV than in newspapers or newsmagazines.

The Active Media

Our analysis of news coverage explored framing and story syntax as well as distribution of coverage. As in the media agenda, we found that media differences were muted by overall agreement. Story framing was particularly uniform. Star Wars and South Africa were reported as conflict, the stock market as an economic issue, and drug abuse and AIDS in terms of human interest. The framing data reinforce culturalist theories of news—that is, that news is grounded in and molds social values (Tuchman, 1978; Gans, 1979; Gusfield, 1981; Robinson and Levy, 1986; Abramson, Arterton, and Orren, 1988).

Syntactical structure revealed quantifiable differences in the way journalists in different media approached the same stories. Although our analysis is only preliminary, given the number of cases in our sample, we found that television journalism puts a heavy emphasis on framing at the initial stages of a story. Some of this may reflect the scene-setting conveyed first by the anchor and then by the reporter, but it may also typify television's attempt to consolidate interest in a story early on. Newsmagazines do less early framing but provide (often conflicting) opinions about problems in the first part of the story. This counterpoint may have a similar arousal effect. Newspapers, as expected, typically emphasize facts, and they provide analysis early in the story. Conceivably, the opening emphasis on new facts may explain why the newspaper story is more challenging to the reader, especially to a less informed reader, than news presentations on television and in magazines.

The area in which media differences were most pronounced, however, involved mostly subjective dimensions which our audience evaluators were able to measure in a unique way. Our findings echo those of other researchers, such as Robinson and Levy, that television is a medium that appeals to emotions and grabs attention. Although the audience-judges recognized the greater analytic qualities of magazines and the emphasis on facts in newspapers, they insisted that TV visuals helped them to learn about all of the topics.

The differences we found in the presentation of news and the construction of meaning by the audience have important implications for the role of the news media in a democratic society. Because the competing demands of family and work make the process of political learning circumscribed and haphazard, the interest-attention dynamic of news becomes critical to connecting the public and private sphere. People care about war and peace, but primarily about the war and peace of their own country. People care about the economy. But some larger issues—race relations in South Africa, the new technologies of Star Wars, or the relationship between the trade deficit and the budget deficit—carry a low interest quotient. In contrast, other issues, such as drug abuse, are high salience issues. Of course, as we have shown, the media have their priorities as well. Issues are more or less prominent in different media—the stock market, for example, is covered religiously in the newspaper, and television gave rioting in South Africa plenty of visual space as long as it was able. But the news media have not provided much prominence to either drug abuse or AIDS. The disjuncture between the salience of issues to the audience and their prominence and coverage in the news media draws attention to the alternative nonmedia sources that people use to construct political reality.

Emphasizing the constructionist tradition in political communications research helps to identify how the news media might be more effective in the democratic process. Constructionism assumes an active role for both the audience and the press. Theories of the press, like those of the audience, can be arranged along an active-passive dimension. On the active side, social responsibility theory holds that the press, if necessary, in conjunction with government, should be engaged in building a more pluralist and more tolerant society (Siebert, Peterson, and Schramm, 1956). This approach puts a great deal of faith in the power of the media to change behavior and make us better. On the passive side, is the cafeteria-line model of communications—the media dish out the news and the public takes what it wants. The press have no special mission in this approach, since most people have no interest in what the press is conveying.

The constructionist perspective emphasizes that the character of the topic of communication is critical to the effectiveness of the communication. For low salience issues, a press that is concerned about its role in the democratic process would want to arouse the attention of the citizenry. For high salience issues, especially those that have a long agenda history, the press may play a different role, drawing attention to new solutions, multiperspectival views, historical context, or economic impact.

Constructing Reality

To emphasize that the audience plays an active role in the communications process is not merely to recognize (as did media commentators as early as Bryce) that no communication "falls on virgin soil," or that everyone is "more or less biased" to begin with. Bryce's position might be called the "warp and woof" view of the audience—that is, the idea that the media must contend with some predictable, demographic bumps on the tabula rasa. In the constructionist perspective, we see individuals select items for attention, reject or ignore topics, redefine terms, infer meaning, draw parallels, and make connections.

This process may sound a great deal like the role of the journalist. In fact, in an intimate observational study of American journalism, Tuchman describes the news process in constructionist terms. She emphasizes how reporters and editors frame stories both in text and pictures, and how those frames organize the "reality" that is presented in the news story (Tuchman, 1978, chap. 9). Gans, who also engaged in a penetrating observational study, presents a somewhat different view. He sees news "as information which is transmitted from sources to audiences, with journalists—who are both employees of bureaucratic commercial organizations and members of a profession—summarizing, refining and altering what becomes available to them from sources in order to make the information suitable for their audiences" (Gans, 1979, p. 80). Gans emphasizes the role of sources in the news process in making stories "available" for news, that is, in making news accessible to the journalist, and the judgments of reporters and editors in making "suitable" news available to the audience. Our constructionist model of communications elaborates on what Gans describes as a circular model by emphasizing that all of the key players in the process are engaged in the construction of reality. Sources (government spokesmen, public affairs people, campaign managers, candidates, and officials) interpret news for reporters. They give the story a "spin" congenial with their goals, and hope to see their construction of reality incorporated into the news story. Journalists reconstruct reality for the audience, taking into account their organizational and modality constraints, professional judgments, and certain expectations about the audience. Finally, the individual reader or viewer constructs a version of reality built from personal experience, interaction with peers, and interpreted selections from the mass media. We do not mean to suggest that the audience is drawing on the same factual base, intimate understanding, or profound interest in the political as the "active 5 percent"—the spin-doctors, journalists, officials, or scholars (Bryce, 1891; Converse, 1964; Diamond and Bates, 1984), but the mental process of constructing a political reality involves the same on-going activities.

Emphasizing that the audience is an active player in the communications process provides both reassurance and opportunity for journalists. As we have seen from our depth interviews, the news is not particularly responsible for the racist or homophobic themes we found in depth interviews concerning South Africa or AIDS. Nor do the news media have to remind the audience that they are a business and that the news is selected to help sell advertising space. These are themes that the audience supplies on its own in framing and constructing political reality. Given this active audience, journalists have something to work with in presenting pictures of the outside world. The public is not merely ballast for the ship of state. Our experimental findings demonstrate that virtually everyone can and does learn something from the news media. Journalists have a responsibility to recognize and augment the capacity of the audience to learn politically relevant information and to make thoughtful political judgments.

The Lessons of Research

In a practical sense, communications research has something to offer journalists. The better we understand how different audiences construct meaning from media reports in different issue domains, the better journalists can, within the constraints of the medium, tailor effective news delivery. One of the lessons of these findings for journalists is that when they are reporting topics for which it is reasonable to expect low levels of attention from significant portions, or even most, of the audience, they may wish to include features in their stories likely to attract attention. Given current levels of interest in foreign, national, and economic news, a great deal more creativity is required in the presentation of less salient news stories.

Because the constraints of media are different, less of an effort to attract attention is made in print than in broadcasting. The rule for television news is, "keep the audience warm for prime time." Producers aim for a consistent level of interest throughout the broadcast and especially in the opening and final segments (Epstein, 1973; Gans, 1979). Print media have different expectations. With a large news hole and a commitment to "all the news," newspapers offer a smorgasbord of items and allow the readers' tastes and interests to guide consumption. It is assumed that most people will not read all of the articles and often will not read to the end of the articles selected (hence the inverted pyramid). Therefore, it makes sense to write print stories addressed to those already "in the know." Given the structure of the news package in various media, therefore, it should come as no surprise that newspapers are less likely to "grab attention" on low salience stories or that television should do so successfully. Since people tend to use a mix of media, if newspapers and magazines did more to capture interest in low-salience stories, the result would reinforce the necessarily brief but dense TV coverage.

At the other end of the continuum are stories about high salience issues. These stories do not need a lot of fanfare. In fact, the human interest angle may even be distracting. We found, for example, that there was a notably low level of learning in a television story on AIDS which opened with a controversy over custody rights between two parents, one of whom tested HIV positive. The distraction of the narrative apparently preoccupied viewers and blocked the recommendations of the National Academy of Sciences, which was the primary focus of the story. While personalizing a story may be good for interest arousal, it may retard the process of accumulating new information. Issues with high levels of audience interest may be more effectively communicated with more context and hard news and less in the way of tangential human vignettes.

While each of the media may be able to redesign coverage in the light of audience response, there may be other ways to reinforce messages. Perhaps the cross-ownership prohibitions discourage a real attempt to get people to follow up news from a lively television presentation into print. If stories in different media were designed to reinforce information, there would be a greater gain from the media mix that individuals already employ in news surveillance.

Given the unevenness that an honest appraisal reveals about our own interests in public affairs (not even news junkies are equally interested in Bulgaria and Peru, in scientific discoveries and corporate mergers), we should be aiming for a mix in our news resources, so that even if journalists do not or cannot provide attention-grabbing devices or contextual clues to match our individual interest profile, we are likely to get what we need from the media that specialize in those effects. A mix of print and broadcasting, in fact, reflects the news habits of 56 percent of the adult public, and only 10 percent rely on television alone (Gollin and Bloom, 1985). While we have often addressed advice about multiple sources to people who rely exclusively on TV, the same message might be usefully conveyed to readers who rely exclusively on an interest-directed medium, such as newspapers. A balanced news diet will help to pique an individual's interest in an expanding range of topics as well as deepening one's understanding of critical issues.

Further research will take us in the direction of natural information gathering and will include the non-news sources that people rely on in daily life to construct meaning about topics in the public arena. Our study of learning continues to impress us with the fact that the news audience is not in a classroom. The motivation, concentration, and pedagogical aids of the teaching environment are not there to help the citizen learn about public affairs. Instead, individuals must incorporate learning about public affairs in the interstices of their private lives. A point that may be less obvious is that journalists are also not in a classroom. They do not have the advantage of teachers when they try to convey information to the audience. They cannot see the eyes that glaze over, the attention that wanders, or the look of puzzlement on their "students'" faces. Their feedback comes almost exclusively from other journalists and occasionally from editors or irate readers. Given the professional structure of journalism, only research undertaken for the purpose is likely to provide the data and the motivation to make news presentation useful to a democratic public. It is to that end that this study is dedicated.

An Appendix on Method

The purpose of this appendix is to provide a more detailed discussion of the multimethod approach we used to examine individuals' construction of political understanding. Specific examples of content analysis category structures, interview protocols, sampled media coverage, and experimental questionnaires are provided. We start with the content analyses. This is followed by sections on the in-depth interviews, the selection of the stories used in the experimental studies, and finally the experimental designs.

The Content Analyses

The general aim of the content analyses was to discern similarities and differences in media coverage of issues that might affect learning from news. Because the selection of issues and stories used in the experiments was not random but purposive, due to the need for parallel information, it was important to be sure that the media differences that we found in the stories used in the experiments represented characteristic differences in media style and not aberrations of the sample. Therefore, a set of objective tests of news content was carried out, both on the stories in the experiments and on a three-year sample of media coverage of the five issues, as indicated in table A.1. Each of the analytic procedures is elaborated below.

Presentational Analysis, Issue Frames, and Differences across Media

All of the experimental stimulus stories as well as the three-year sample of news stories were content analyzed by trained coders. Content analysis measures included the numbers of words, pictures, and human interest vignettes in the story; references to various people and

Table A.1   Content Analyses of Media Coverage

	Media Agenda	Present-ational Analysis	Issue Frame Analysis	Structural Syntax
Experimental story sample ($N = 30$) (3 media, 5 issues, 2 stories per issue)	No	Yes	Yes	Yes
Five-issue sample ($N = 150$) (3 media, 5 issues, 10 stories per issue)	Yes	Yes	Yes	No
All issue samples (14 media, all issues, all stories, 1985–87)	Yes	No	No	No

groups, including experts, political actors in the United States and abroad, and the American public; the frequency of expository factors, such as definitions, explanations of causes, consequences, possible solutions, and governmental policy; and an analysis of the way issues were framed in the news stories. There were no statistically significant differences across media in any of the measures, with one exception. Newspapers contained more than twice as many statements from and about people as did television or newsmagazines: the means are 18.0, 7.5, and 6.0, respectively, with F significant at .035. Thus, in terms of the content elements associated with news production, the stimulus stories are statistically similar across media and they are consistent with coverage found in the same media over a three-year period.

Stimulus versus Sample Media Coverage

Table A.2 demonstrates that the pattern of variance in the stimulus stories is similar to that of the large sample of stories drawn from the same media over a three-year period. The differences in means between the stimulus stories and the three-year sample for each of the content analysis variables are statistically insignificant. The means are similar for both the attention/involvement factors and the context/expository factors.

Additionally, there are few statistically significant media differences between the stimulus and sample stories when each issue is ex-

Table A.2   Comparison of Means of the Stimulus Stories
and the Three-Year Sample of Media Coverage

	Stimulus Stories ($N = 30$)	3-Year Sample ($N = 150$)	Significance of F
Attention/involvement factors:			
Number of pictures	10.1	8.6	.59
Human interest	1.5	1.2	.34
References to specific people	7.3	8.7	.54
Context/expository factors:			
Number of words	768	720	.59
Expert sources	7.1	6.1	.59
Causes	5.5	4.8	.49
Consequences	7.0	8.1	.55
Definitions	1.6	1.5	.22
Policy references	5.0	3.6	.16

amined separately. The differences that did arise were not consistent across issues and are probably best attributed to random variation. Several content categories were significantly different in the drug and AIDS newspaper stories, in both of which the stimulus stories contained more references to people than did the sample stories. This seems to be due to the longer average length of the stimulus stories selected for these two issues, which was necessary to assure similar coverage of the issues by all three media.

Structural Syntax

The presentational and frame analyses tell us what is available in each media story, but do not tell us anything about the order of presentation of information, which may vary substantially across media. We conducted an analysis of the structural syntax of the media by noting the ordering and style of presentation in each media story. Each story used in the experiments was read for its use of scene-setting or framing remarks, facts, opinions and affective statements, and analysis. For example, the first few paragraphs of the newspaper story on Benjamin Moloise were coded as a statement of the problem (frame) followed by five factual statements and concluding with a moralizing and directive message from Moloise.

Excerpt from *Boston Globe*

PRETORIA—Benjamin Moloise, a black nationalist
guerilla and poet, was hanged in maximum-security Pre-   framing
toria Central Prison early today despite pleas worldwide
for clemency and threats of bloody reprisals.

Moloise, 30, had been sentenced to death for the
shooting of Warrant Officer Phillipus Selepe, a black se-   fact
curity policeman, during an ambush near Pretoria in
1982.

Among those who held a vigil outside the prison
awaiting Moloise's death was his mother, Mamike Mo-   fact
loise, who arrived a few minutes before the scheduled
hanging supported by two friends. Police with dogs kept   fact
watch outside the pale stone walls of the newly completed maximum-security facility.

Yesterday, Mamike Moloise met with her son in   fact
prison for the last time and carried back a message to
South Africa's disenfranchised blacks that 'freedom is   opinion
at hand.'

'Tomorrow I will spill my blood for those who remain
behind. The struggle must go on, nobody must fear it.'   opinion

The Depth Interviews

The depth interviews were designed to explore how individuals and
journalists understand and communicate about political issues. The
journalist interviews are described in Chapter 2 (for more detail, see
Kiolbassa, 1989). Two waves of interviews were conducted with a
random subsample of the experimental subjects. The initial interviews
were conducted in November 1987 with twenty-seven people. The
second wave of interviews was conducted in order to assess the stability over time and across issues of the frames used to discuss political
topics. See table A.3. Twenty-nine people were interviewed during the
second wave in August 1988. Thirteen of these were re-interviews and
covered two topics that had been discussed earlier and two topics that
had not. The remaining sixteen interviews were with people who had
not previously been interviewed. In all, forty-three different people
were interviewed: seventeen men and twenty-six women ranging in
age from eighteen to eighty-seven.

In order to minimize the interviewer's role and maximize the indi-

Table A.3   Number of In-Depth Interviews

	South Africa	SDI	Crash	Drugs	AIDS	Total
Depth interviews	33	37	16	34	35	43
Re-interviews	5	6	13	4	6	13

vidual's expression of thoughts and feelings, the interview protocol was based as much or more on listening and encouraging conversation as it was on directing questions and probes. Interviewers used six general questions to initiate conversation on the four randomly selected topics as follows:

There are lots of current events. It would certainly be difficult to follow each one in detail. We're just interested in what you think.

1.   If you had to explain the general idea of _____ to someone who doesn't know about it, how would you explain it?

   Anything else?

   Are there any images or pictures that come into your mind when you think about that issue?

2.   How do you feel about _____?

   What did you think about when you told me how you feel?

   How did you come to have that opinion?

3.   How did you find out about _____?

   (How do you know about)

PROBE HERE FOR SPECIFIC SOURCES PEOPLE USE

4.   How do the media treat this issue?

   Why do you think the media cover this issue?

5.   How important to you personally is this issue?

   How important to the country is this issue?

6.   Is this issue like any other that you can think of? How so?

REPEAT FOR EACH OF THE FOUR ISSUES.

7.   Finally, I would like you to rank the issues in order of their importance to you personally and then to the country.

The interviews were transcribed and analyzed for the frames people
used to talk about the issues. It was often difficult to separate out the
frames from just a few words, because individuals often used several
frames to discuss one issue or spoke at length to communicate the
frame. The following excerpt from an interview with a twenty-one-
year-old woman illustrates some of these problems and how she
framed the issues of drug abuse and AIDS in terms of human impact
and empathy, morality, and also in terms of the individual's lack of
control over events. As Gamson's work emphasizes, the full transcripts illustrate how interpersonal conversations/anecdotes/jokes,
fragments from entertainment and news media coverage, national statistics, and personal life experiences are integrated together almost
seamlessly in the individual's thinking about public issues (Gamson,
1992).

Q: Is this issue (drug abuse) like any other that you can
think of?

A: Well, it's kind of like AIDS to an extent, but drugs is
kind of . . . it is your own fault unless someone, you know,
someone keeps putting drugs or heroin in your cigarette or
something like that and you're addicted to it all of a sudden
because you got it. That's not your fault. But drugs is, most
of the time, someone's own fault. They try it and then get
some more and get some more and get some more. Where
AIDS isn't necessarily the person's fault. You know. I don't
think it is. Because I know someone who died of AIDS. He
doesn't know who the hell he got it from. You know, that's
not his fault. Everyone has sex. You don't expect someone to
have sex with you and give you AIDS. You know, it's just all
of a sudden, everyone's getting it. And they're centering it on
homosexuals which I think is unfair.
   I heard a story that the first AIDS cases were two guys in
New York, I don't know how true the story is, this is what I
heard. There were two guys in New York and they went to the
doctor and the doctor wouldn't see them, treat them or something like that and that was one of the first cases of AIDS. But

the doctor just wouldn't do anything about it. And now everyone is getting it.

But people are misled about it. I went to bingo with this woman, and she's very educated about everything. And this man was sneezing at bingo, you know, he's one of the guys . . . and she goes, she calls me Kay. And she goes, "Kay, if he had AIDS, we'd all have it now." I says, go on the guy's just sneezing. She goes, "oh, no, no, no if he had AIDS we'd all have it now, it's in this room." I said, "why don't you read up on it a little?" You know, we ended up getting into an argument about it because I knew I was right and she thought she was right and we just argued about and I said, "whatever Helen, just read up on it or something—talk to me when you know what you're talking about." You know, I thought that was ridiculous, the guy sneezed, everyone would be dead. Everyone sneezes. Crazy world. People don't know what they're talking about but they talk about it anyways.

(Here the interviewer breaks the silence by asking the interviewee to explain the idea of AIDS to somebody who didn't know about it.)

A: Well. The majority of it is centered around homosexuals and bisexuals and I.V. drug users. And in turn, I find it, a lot of prostitutes are going to start spreading it. Because if someone has AIDS, I know a lot of people must feel resentful because . . . it's like . . . now they don't know who they got it from. It could be a handful of people who could've had it. So, they're going to start going to prostitutes or anyone, raping people just so that they can have sex. That's their way of getting back whoever gave it to them. So, I just tell people to make sure you know who you're having sex with. No more one night stands or these bar flings you know. No one's ugly after two, you know what I mean? No more of that stuff. You have to know who you're having sex with. That's why I'm so glad I'm married. I don't have to worry about that. I have a girlfriend and she has herpes. She got it from her boyfriend who got it from some girl he fooled around with. Now she's got it for the rest of her life. That's not going to kill her. She's lucky it was only herpes, it could've been AIDS. She could be dead right now. People just have to watch who they go with and definitely stay away from people who are into drugs. I mean look it, people from drugs are affecting the

AIDS people now. You know, they're affecting that. Stay away from people who are into drugs.

I know a lot of people who are gay. Gay people are very safe sex now. I think the smart ones. You know, there's dumb in every group, religion, race whatever. There are stupid people in everything. I just say (pause) I wouldn't have sex with anyone who is bisexual if you knew they were bisexual. I don't care if it's your long lost love, stay away from it because it wouldn't be worth it. Your life's over. Was it worth it? I don't think it would be. Just have safe sex and (pause) and if you are going to have sex with someone you don't know too well, get rubbers and (pause) I think the spermicides help and just keep up with the stuff and you know, don't let anyone . . . So, I'd just be extra cautious with everything. Everything.

If I needed blood, I'd go to my mother or my sister. It's like they said the other day, some contaminated blood . . . from back . . . it was either 1972 or 1976 up until recently they found out some of it was contaminated with AIDS. Get blood from immediate family that is not gay, bisexual or ever was an I.V. drug user because they might not even know yet. You know, the incubation period could last quite awhile. I'd say, stick with a select group of friends, you know, because you could go out with people you don't know and get raped. Anything could happen. Some people will, you know, drug you. You know, shoot you up with drugs. I saw it on . . . even though it was on a soap opera, I'm sure it's happened, they knew this guy used to be into drugs and he owed him something and they kept shooting him . . . he was into cocaine, they booted it you know, made it liquid and kept shooting him up with it and then . . . A funny thing, he thought he had AIDS on the show. And you know, you watch the show everyday even though it just fantasy world. All of a sudden, Mark Dalton on *All My Children* thinks he has AIDS and it's like . . . wow that's right, he used to be an I.V. drug user. And I hadn't even thought of that. Well, he didn't end up having it but it kind of put a scare into him for about three weeks for the . . . (inaudible).

But with AIDS, I would be straight, blunt. Because not everyone does drugs. I mean, not everyone . . . yeah, most people do drugs or have tried it. But they subside. They don't do it a wicked lot, you know, they might go on sprees. And you got people who are really into it. But like me, I don't do drugs. And I don't think you do drugs. But everyone has sex at some point. Hopefully, everyone wants to at least you know? Everyone wants sex and they need it. I mean, people have sex hopefully, more than they do drugs. You know, I'm talking everyone in general. Like my mother, she doesn't do drugs but she has sex. Everyone has sex. So it's something more common.

That Helen, as a matter of fact, I talked to her today. What did she tell . . . you should hear this one. This one was about AIDS. She said, "This year." Now I'll remind you this is only November, there is only one more month left of this year. She goes, "You know, in this year more people are going to die of AIDS than people who were killed in Vietnam and Korea combined." I said, "Oh really? That's a new interesting story you have for me Helen. Did you read that one?" She goes, "Yeah, no kidding, Kay, no kidding. More people are going to die of AIDS this year than people who died in Vietnam and the Korean War." That's very interesting, it makes you think, doesn't it? But, I don't believe anything she says, you know? Because it's uneducated Helen. She's nice, just don't talk serious to her. And don't tell her anything that you don't want repeated. If you want someone to something, tell her. It will be around.

And for pictures in my mind about AIDS, would be that guy I know that died. I used to be good friends with him and he got it and he exposed someone I know to it. This person . . . after he died . . . this friend of mine . . . he went and they were doing like, it was like two or three years ago, and they asked him . . . because you know doctors and everything, they knew he had AIDS. They asked him if he would be in like a survey so that they could, not experiment with him, but like check his blood and check his weight and you know, keep an eye on him because he hasn't broken out yet with it or come down with it. They just want to keep an eye on him and they said that he was definitely exposed. So now he's living in fear.

The Experiments
The Audience Evaluation Study

In addition to the content analyses as described above, the media stories used in the experiments were also evaluated by a panel of 150 audience evaluators, who were drawn from the same population of mall shoppers as the subjects in the experiments. The evaluators were asked to read or view four stories (two stories for each of two issues) in one medium. After each story, the participants answered open-ended questions about the main points of the story and the use of visuals, questions about the primary themes or frames of the stories, and a series of 7-point-scale questions that delved into their evaluations of the stories. There were two basic scale question stems: the first, "Was this story . . ." and the second, "How much did this story tell you about. . ." For example, a scale value of 1 meant that a story was not at all interesting, whereas a score of 7 meant that the story was very interesting. The words associated with each question are listed in table A.4.

Selecting News Stories for the Experiments

Selecting parallel issue coverage from each medium on a range of issues turned out to be more difficult than we had expected, especially given the accepted view that topics are covered similarly in various media. By using news indices and reviewing many stories, we eventually selected a purposive sample of two similar stories on each issue from each of the television, newspaper, and newsmagazine sources. A complete list of the thirty stories used in the experiments is included in table A.5.

Table A.4   Content Evaluation Study Scale Words

Was this story . . .	How much did this story tell you about . . .
Interesting	People
Clear	Conflicts
Relevant to you	Reporter's own views
Relevant to the U.S.	Facts
Emotionally involving	Causes of the issue
Hard to understand	Effects of the issue
Complicated	Possible solutions
Attention-grabbing	Moral values
Confusing	Politics of the issue
Human interest	History of the issue
Frightening	Economics of the issue
Routine	People in control of issue
	What people can do
	Mistrust in U.S. government

Table A.5   Experimental Story Sample ($N = 30$)

	TV	Magazines	Boston Globe
South Africa			
Moloise	10/18/85	10/28/85	10/18/85
Press curb	11/02/85	12/02/85	10/31/85
SDI			
Weapons	11/11/85	10/27/86*‡	11/04/85
Commercials	11/14/85	12/09/85	12/10/85
Crash			
Causes	11/02/87†	11/02/87	10/25/87
Impact	10/20/87†	11/02/87‡	10/20/87
Drugs			
Crack	12/04/85	09/15/86	06/29/86
Cocaine	12/30/85	01/20/86	07/01/86
AIDS			
NAS report	10/29/86	11/10/86	10/30/86
Testing	02/24/87	03/02/87	02/25/87

Note: All television stories were from *CBS Evening News* and all newsmagazine stories were from *Time* magazine with the following exceptions: * *US News and World Report,* † *ABC World News Tonight,* and ‡ *Newsweek.*

The chief concern was to identify stories which contained the same basic information across all media. At the level of the individual story, however, the task was made quite difficult by variation across media, due in part to different journalistic practices and styles. As an example of the parallel content, we have cited below excerpts from the television, magazine, and newspaper versions of the death of Benjamin Moloise in South Africa. Dan Rather introduced the television report by mentioning briefly the hanging and then immediately alluding to subsequent violence in Johannesburg.

DAN RATHER: South Africa today turned a defiant deaf ear to worldwide calls for clemency and hanged a 28-year-old black poet for killing a policeman. John Blackstone reports that within hours some whites were running for their lives in the streets of downtown Johannesburg.

JOHN BLACKSTONE: The execution of Benjamin Moloise was answered with raised fists and songs of revolution. Moloise's mother joined hundreds expressing not sorrow, but defiance. Winnie Mandela was there defying the law. The wife of the jailed black leader, Nelson Mandela, is prohibited from appearing at public gatherings.

WINNIE MANDELA: We need you all, to join hands, and fight.

JOHN BLACKSTONE: After the meeting, the defiance spilled into the streets. When police first attempted to break up the demonstration, blacks fought back. Two policemen were injured, one seriously. The police then seemed unwilling or unable to control the crowd. Suddenly, whites in the center of Johannesburg began to experience the anger and violence that until now has been largely contained in the black townships. Passing whites were taunted and chased. The windows of white-owned shops were smashed and looted. At times, the police seemed helpless, running from the black onslaught. Then, there was a gun shot. One man was wounded. Police accused him of looting. Still, the lawlessness did not end. It was three hours before peace was restored in the heart of the city. (*CBS Evening News,* October 18, 1985).

Initially, Blackstone's voice-over was accompanied by video of an indoor meeting of blacks listening to Winnie Mandela speak. As Blackstone shifted to discuss the demonstrations, the visuals moved outside and showed crowds of blacks running and breaking store windows, while white police chased them. A single white male was shown swinging a handcuff at a crowd of black men who had encircled him; a white couple scurried down the street ducking their heads and seeking shelter. The visuals then shifted quickly to more blacks breaking windows and looting, followed by a sudden camera jump to a black man writhing in pain with several white police standing over him. The first part of the story was then resolved and the visuals showed a Johannesburg street returned to the usual stream of passing cars and pedestrians.

The newspaper and magazine stories were somewhat different, because they provided a broader context for Moloise's execution. The *Boston Globe* story was published without pictures under the headline, "Black poet Benjamin Moloise is executed in South Africa."

PRETORIA—Benjamin Moloise, a black nationalist guerilla and poet, was hanged in maximum-security Pretoria Central Prison early today despite pleas worldwide for clemency and threats of bloody reprisals. Moloise, 30, had been sentenced to death for the shooting of Warrant Officer Phillipus Selepe, a black security policeman, during an ambush near Pretoria in 1982. Among those who held a vigil outside the prison awaiting Moloise's death was his mother, Mamike Moloise, who arrived a few minutes before the scheduled hanging supported by two friends. Police with dogs kept watch outside the pale stone walls of the newly completed maximum-security facility.

Yesterday, Mamike Moloise met with her son in prison for the last time and carried back a message to South Africa's disenfranchised blacks that "freedom is at hand." "Tomorrow I will spill my blood for those who remain behind. The struggle must go on, nobody must fear it." The outlawed African National Congress has taken responsibility for the slaying and said Moloise was not part of the hit team.

In a statement issued from its headquarters in Lusaka, Zambia, the ANC said that if Moloise was executed, his death would be avenged "in every corner of our land." In Cape Town, the United Democratic Front, the main group fighting apartheid, said: "The legalized murder of a young man who is seen as a hero and patriot by many South Africans will only fuel mass anger."

In Woodstock, a white suburb of Cape Town, youths broke shop windows after a day of widespread unrest in which police repeatedly fired shotguns and tear gas at rioters . . . (*Boston Globe,* October 18, 1985).

Time magazine's coverage focused on events surrounding Moloise's hanging and was published with one photograph of black men overturning a van during disturbances in the Cape Town suburb of Athlone, even though this event was only mentioned in the final paragraph of the story. The headline in *Time* was a quote from one of Moloise's writings, " 'I Am Proud to Give My Life': The execution of a poet touches off an angry rampage."

The government had been warned that hanging Benjamin Moloise, 30, a black upholsterer and poet, would lead to bloodshed. The U.S. had asked State President P. W. Botha to "take another look" at the planned execution. The Soviet Union, the European Community, the 49-nation Commonwealth of Britain and the U.N. Security Council, among others, had also asked that Moloise's life be spared. But Botha refused all appeals for clemency, and last week, shortly after dawn, Moloise went to the gallows at Pretoria Central Prison. In Washington, White House Spokesman Larry Speakes told reporters: "We hoped that this action would not be taken."

In Johannesburg, which has so far been spared serious racial violence, news of the hanging was greeted with outrage. After a noontime memorial service for Moloise, hundreds of blacks poured into the streets of the city's white downtown area and went on a four-hour rampage. Two policemen were stabbed and about a dozen white pedestrians were robbed or beaten, one of them severely. At least ten shops were looted. Police made six arrests and shot one suspect in the leg.

Moloise had been convicted two years ago of murdering a black policeman. The victim, Warrant Officer Phillipus Selepe, 52, was slain with an automatic weapon outside his home near Pretoria in 1982. Moloise at first confessed the crime but later recanted, charging police coercion. Later he said he had been involved in planning the ambush, but only because he was afraid that his associates in the African National Congress would kill him if he did not cooperate. The A.N.C., for its part, has insisted that its guerrillas, not Moloise, committed the murder. Moloise was, however, a firm supporter of the A.N.C. and the violent overthrow of apartheid. As he once wrote: "A storm of oppression will be followed by the rain of my blood/ I am proud to give my life, my solitary life."

Following the execution, Mamike Moloise, 53, complained bitterly that she had been denied the opportunity to visit her son on the day of his death. "I begged," said the bereaved mother, who waited outside the prison gates accompanied by, among others, Winnie Mandela, wife of jailed A.N.C. leader Nelson Mandela. "I said, It's the last time. That's my son. This government is cruel. It is really, really cruel." Mrs. Moloise was later permitted to see her son's unopened coffin, but his body will remain the property of the state and will be buried inside the prison in a grave marked by a number . . . (*Time,* October 28, 1985).

As one can see from even a casual reading of the above stories, the ordering of information, relative emphasis, and visual reinforcement of information may vary significantly at the level of the individual story. It draws attention to the inherent difficulty in experimental research of this kind in generalizing from the micro to the macro level about the nature of potential media and modality effects.

The Media and Modality Experiments

The procedures for the cross media and modality experiments are described in detail in Chapter 2. Here we will focus on the measures used to assess two of our key variables: cognitive skill and prior knowledge. The subjects' cognitive skill was assessed by using two standardized tests from the Factor Referenced Cognitive Inventory developed by the Educational Testing Service. These were the Advanced Vocabulary Test, Part I, and the Inference Test, Part I. Vocabulary tests are often used as shorthand cognitive assessments but we have found them particularly apt for measuring the capacity to understand news coverage. The ability to draw inferences is also important to understanding the news, since the norm of brevity in journalism means that

Table A.6   Exemplary Measures from the Cognitive Skills Tests

Vocabulary Test Items:
    emergence 1-laziness 2-identity 3-contrast 4-coming forth
    decadence 1-decline 2-decision 3-color 4-joy
    furlough 1-leave of absence 2-garden 3-foot soldier 4-timberland
    exonerate 1-betray 2-transgress 3-exult 4-vindicate

Inference Test Items:
1. More fatal accidents occur on highways after dark than during daylight hours.
    a. Darkness causes many accidents.
    b. A decrease in the volume of traffic tends to increase fatal accidents.
    c. The chance of being killed in an automobile accident is lower during the day than it is at night.
    d. There are more fatal accidents after dark since drivers tend to be more tired.
    e. After dark, drivers frequently have accidents when they are blinded by the lights of oncoming cars.
2. One year a particular farmer's stand of wheat yielded 40 bushels per acre.
    a. The farmer's land is extremely fertile.
    b. The farmer has raised wheat on his land.
    c. The weather that year was unfavorable for growing wheat.
    d. Forty bushels per acre is a high yield.
    e. The field would be more suitable for some other crop.

Source: The Educational Testing Service.

Table A.7   General Media Usage Questions

---

1) What is your primary source of news? (Please check one.)

   TV   newspaper   magazine   radio   other people
   other (please specify)

2) About how often do you follow the national network news on television?

   every day   3–4 times   1–2 times   1–2 times   never
                a week   a week   a month

3) About how often do you follow the news in the newspaper?

   every day   3–4 times   1–2 times   1–2 times   never
                a week   a week   a month

4) About how often do you follow the news in newsmagazines?

   every day   2–3 times   once a   1–2 times   never
                a week   month   a year

5) All other things being equal, how would you prefer to get most of your news?

   TV   newspaper   magazine   radio   other people
   other (please specify)

Specific Media Usage Questions

7) What is your primary source of news about apartheid in South Africa?

   TV   newspaper   magazine   radio   other people
   other (please specify)

8) How much attention would you say you've paid to news about apartheid in
   South Africa.

   1   2   3   4   5   6   7
   a great deal   none

---

reporters do not elaborate information in fine detail. The cognitive skills tests were administered at the end of each experiment's pretest and helped to distract the subject's attention from the news emphasis of the studies. In fact, many of our subjects thought the cognitive skills tests were some kind of game. Examples of the cognitive skills items are included in table A.6.

We note that all of the experiments led with questions about general media usage as well as attention to the specific issue that was the focus of the experiment. Table A.7 lists the questions that were used to eval-

Table A.8   Exemplary Issue Knowledge Checklist Items, South Africa

---

Do any of the following describe the present situation in South Africa?

Imprisonment of Nelson Mandela	___ yes	___ no	___ don't know
Violent political protests	___ yes	___ no	___ don't know
Separate residential areas for each race	___ yes	___ no	___ don't know
Earthquakes	___ yes	___ no	___ don't know
Demonstrators breaking shop windows and looting	___ yes	___ no	___ don't know
Police brutality	___ yes	___ no	___ don't know

---

uate media usage and that were central to our finding concerning the connection between media usage and cognitive skill.

In order to measure learning, it was necessary to have a baseline measure of each subject's prior knowledge about the issue as well as a measure of post-exposure knowledge. This was accomplished by using an eleven-to-thirteen-item true-false checklist in both the pretest and the post-test. Three steps were taken in order to minimize or account for the presence of the checklist. First, the pretest checklist was separated from the stimulus by a political and personal efficacy inventory, a political participation index, the vocabulary test, and the inference problems. Second, items were added to the post-test version of the checklist. And third, exposure/post-test and post-test only control groups were built into the design of some of the experiments. Examples of some of the checklist items for the issue of apartheid in South Africa are included in table A.8. Items were included in the checklist based on the information contained in the news stories.

Notes

Chapter 1

1. We use the phrase "common knowledge" rather than the more traditional "public opinion" to emphasize three themes in our research: (a) We focus on what the public "knows" about the political world rather than emphasizing gaps in their knowledge of textbook civics; (b) We focus on a more broadly defined "cognition" and "sense-making" of the political world rather than pre-coded opinion-choices; (c) We contrast the "common language" and natural discourse of the mass public with the official "public discourse" of the media.

2. Many serious analyses of these issues share this perspective, from Lippmann (1925), who characterized the goals of journalism as fundamentally "unattainable," to Graber's more recent study of political news (1988), which concludes with a section entitled, "The Impossible Task of the Mass Media."

3. The accumulated literature on issue voting and citizen competence is intimidatingly large, conflicting, and technical. Key contributions to the controversy over time include the following: Downs (1957), Campbell et al. (1960, 1966), Key (1961, 1966), Converse (1964, 1970, 1975), Stokes (1966), Shapiro (1969), Brown (1970), Repass (1971), Brody and Page (1972), Kessel (1972), Pomper (1972), Broh (1973), Pierce and Rose (1974), Kelley and Mirer (1974), Stimson (1975), Achen (1975), Miller et al. (1976), Nie, Verba, and Petrocik (1976), Popkin et al. (1976), Margolis (1977), Bishop, Tuchfarber, and Oldenick (1978), Sullivan, Piereson, and Marcus (1978), Petrocik (1979), Klingemann (1979), Converse and Markus (1979), Markus and Converse (1979), Carmines and Stimson (1980), Judd and Milburn (1980), Pierce and Sullivan (1980), Fiorina (1981), Gant and Davis (1984), Inglehart (1985), Kinder and Sears (1985), Lau and Erber (1985), Bartels (1986), Neuman (1986), Luskin (1987), Bartels (1988), Smith (1989), Ferejohn and Kuklinski (1990), Fiorina (1990), and Zaller (1991).

4. The succession of charges and countercharges so exasperated Philip Converse that he published a little how-to article listing six techniques that could generate and interpret data in such as way as to refute his own seminal

findings on the sometimes ephemeral connection among issue knowledge, issue opinions, and vote decisions in the mass public (Converse, 1980).

5. The constructivist perspective, although similar in spirit, follows a very different research path than our own by focusing on interpersonal rather than mass communication.

6. Turning the question of citizen competence on its head resonates with some of Jean Piaget's early work on human intelligence. Rather than focusing on how subjects came to calculate the "right" answers in the Binet intelligence test, Piaget became fascinated by the logical processes people used in arriving at the "wrong" answers. He felt more was revealed about human cognition by systematically studying how people actually reasoned rather than developing artificial standards and measures of "proper" reasoning. The ramifications of Piaget's challenge to the traditional paradigm of human cognition are discussed in Gardner (1981, 1985) and Rosenberg (1988).

Chapter 2

1. Although virtually all social science research methods texts praise the virtues of the multimethod/multimeasure strategy, the constraints of real-world research continue to make it a relatively rare phenomenon in published research. The model of multimethod research is closely akin to the concepts of convergent validity and the multitrait-multimethod matrix (Campbell and Fiske, 1959), multiple indicators (Blalock, 1982), meta-analysis (Rosenthal, 1991), and multimethod triangulation (Nimmo and Swanson, 1990).

2. In order to isolate the effects of media on learning, other contextual variables had to be controlled. Therefore these experiments do not assess the impact of behavioral, physical, or news context variables on learning.

Chapter 3

1. A small sample of studies (Repass, 1971; McCombs and Shaw, 1972; Gans, 1979; Patterson, 1980; Neuman and Fryling, 1985; Graber, 1988; Jensen, 1988; van Dijk, 1988; Edelstein, Ito, and Kepplinger, 1989) reveals lists of between four and a dozen categories involving variations on nine general issues: politics, economics, international relations/defense, the environment, health, poverty, race relations, crime, and morality. There are variations in labels reflecting the flavor of a particular historical era. McCombs and Shaw, for example, label race as civil rights and crime as law and order. Neuman and Fryling focused on Watergate and Vietnam as key thematic issues for politics and international relations for the era under study. There are variations reflecting the political perspectives of the analyst. Van Dijk, for example, uses the terms pollution, hunger, racism, and disarmament to label categories more generally defined as environment, poverty, race relations, and

international relations, respectively. Graber, because of her particular interest in the crime issue, broke out subcategories of crime, police activities, and corruption. Edelstein, Ito, and Kepplinger, because of their international emphasis, added the categories of overpopulation and trade balance. But overall, the similarities of thematic structure are striking.

2. All references in this section to a percentage of total national and international news coverage devoted to a particular issue are drawn from the Conference on Issues and Media's *National News Index,* 1985–87.

3. The concept of "framing" a news story has diverse uses in social science research (Goffman, 1974; Iyengar, 1991; Tankard et al., 1991). In our discussion we will emphasize two uses of the term: framing as journalists put a news event in a broader social and historical context, and framing as individuals attempt to interpret a news event in terms of their own life space.

Chapter 4

1. Graber (1988) identifies six frames or "thinking categories" which find frequent use by her depth interviewees. Her human interest/empathy category corresponds to our human impact frame, her cultural norms to our morality frame, her institution judgments to our powerlessness category. In addition she has three more overarching categories (simple situation sequence, cause-effect, and person judgments) dealing with styles of causal attribution. Gans (1979) and Gamson (1992) develop typologies of different emphases within the morality and values frame. Iyengar (1991) focuses on how the framing of individual versus social responsibility for different social problems predominates in media coverage and in individual conceptions, an analysis that corresponds to our categories of powerlessness and human impact.

2. Liebes and Crigler (1990) provide further discussion of the range and scope of the conflict theme in a comparative analysis of issue framing in the United States and Israel.

3. Building on Rotter's original work (1966), researchers found at least three aspects to locus of control: an "individual responsibility" factor, a "control by powerful others" factor, and a "control by chance" factor (Collins et al., 1973; Kleiber, Veldman, and Menaker, 1976; Levenson, 1973).

Chapter 5

1. In terms of content, the ratio of hard news to features, human interest, sports, and entertainment is quite similar in both media (Neuman, 1986, p. 136).

2. This formulation can be interpreted as follows: was the difference between the pretest and the post-test score for a particular subject greater than or less than the average difference for the sample in that experiment? The calcula-

tions generate a "residualized change score" with a mean of zero and change measured in standard deviation units of the post-test. Thus a residualized change score of zero would mean that the subject's pretest/post-test difference is equal to the mean for all subjects, a score of 1.5 would represent a difference one and a half standard deviations higher than the sample mean, and so on. All statistical tests were performed on these residualized change scores.

To make the metric of learning more interpretable (that is, more like the original simple change score), in reporting the patterns of learning in descriptive figures and tables we performed one final adjustment, a simple linear transformation so that standard deviations are reported as a percentage of the total items in the index and the sample mean is reset from zero to the original net positive score, again as a percentage of total items. Such a linear transformation, of course, has no effect on the statistical tests and provides a more accessible measure of learning.

Chapter 6

1. Our comparisons of learning across media support the findings of Hoijer, who studied television news. She discovered that manipulating the television stories to increase the amount of contextual information resulted in greater audience comprehension of the stories. Her research was remarkable in that it involved the manipulation of actual television news broadcasts to emphasize different aspects of the news story—e.g., who, what, where, and why—as well as various forms of illustration, including text headlining. She stresses that whatever the form of illustration, contextualizing the story with cause and effect results in greater information gain (Hoijer, 1984, 1990).

Chapter 7

1. Note that we refer here not to education but to cognitive skill. Education reduces but does not eliminate the relationship between TV-dependence and political knowledge. When the research setting allows, the measurement of cognitive skill independent of educational level helps to sort out the causal processes.

References

Abel, Elie. 1981. "The First Word." In Elie Abel, ed., *What's News*, pp. 3–9. San Francisco: Institute for Contemporary Studies.

Abramson, Jeffrey B., F. Christopher Arterton, and Gary R. Orren. 1988. *The Electronic Commonwealth: The Impact of New Media Technologies on Democratic Politics*. New York: Basic Books.

Achen, Christopher. 1975. "Mass Political Attitudes and the Survey Response." *American Political Science Review* 69:1218–31.

Alger, Dean. 1987. "Television, Perceptions of Reality and the Electoral Process." Annual Meeting of the American Political Science Association. Chicago.

Altheide, David L. 1976. *Creating Reality: How TV News Distorts Events*. Newbury Park, Calif.: Sage.

Andriate, Gregory S., and Michael J. Beatty. 1988. "Cognitive Complexity and Cognitive Backlog in Human Information Processing." In Brent Ruben, ed., *Information and Behavior*. New Brunswick, N.J.: Transaction.

Arterton, Christopher, Edward H. Lazarus, John Griffen, and Monica C. Andres. 1984. "Telecommunications Technologies and Political Participation." Report to the Markle Foundation, Roosevelt Center. Washington, D.C.

Atkin, C. K., J. Galloway, and O. Nayman. 1976. "News Media Exposure, Political Knowledge, and Campaign Interest." *Journalism Quarterly* 53:231–37.

Babbie, Earl. 1973. *Survey Research Methods*. Belmont, Calif.: Wadsworth.

Bagdikian, Ben H. 1983. *The Media Monopoly*. Boston: Beacon Press.

Ball-Rokeach, Sandra J. 1985. "The Origins of Individual Media System Dependency: A Sociological Framework." *Communication Research* 12:485–510.

Ball-Rokeach, Sandra J., Gerard F. Power, K. Kendall Guthrie, and H. Ross Waring. 1990. "Value-Framing Abortion in the United States: An Application of Media System Dependency Theory." *International Journal of Public Opinion Research* 2(3):249–73.

Barber, James David. 1978. "Television and the Future of Civic Perception." Annual meeting of the American Political Science Association.

———. 1979. "Not the New York Times: What Network News Should Be." *Washington Monthly* (September), pp. 14–21.

Bard, Mitchell. 1987. "Strategic Thoughts about SDI." *Public Opinion* 9(6):17–19.

Barkin, Steve M., and Michael Gurevitch. 1987. "Out of Work and On the Air: Television News of Unemployment." *Critical Studies in Mass Communication* 4:1–20.

Bartels, Larry. 1986. "Issue Voting under Uncertainty: An Empirical Test." *American Journal of Political Science* 30:709–28.

———. 1988. *Presidential Primaries and the Dynamics of Public Choice.* Princeton: Princeton University Press.

Becker, Lee, and D. Charles Whitney. 1980. "Effects of Media Dependencies." *Communication Research* 7:95–120.

Beentjes, Johannes W. J., and Tom H. A. van der Voort. 1989. "Television and Young People's Reading Behaviour: A Review of Research." *European Journal of Communication* 4(1):51–77.

Bennett, W. Lance. 1988. *News: The Politics of Illusion,* 2d ed. New York: Longman.

Berelson, Bernard, Paul Lazarsfeld, and William McPhee. 1954. *Voting: A Study of Opinion Formation in a Presidential Campaign.* Chicago: University of Chicago Press.

Bishop, George F., Alfred J. Tuchfarber, and Robert W. Oldenick. 1978. "Change in the Structure of American Political Attitudes: The Nagging Question of Question Wording." *American Journal of Political Science* 22:250–69.

Blalock, Hubert M., Jr. 1982. *Conceptualization and Measurement of the Social Sciences.* Beverly Hills: Sage.

Blumler, Jay, and Elihu Katz, eds. 1974. *The Uses of Mass Communications.* Newport Beach: Sage.

Blumler, Jay G., Michael Gurevitch, and Elihu Katz. 1985. "Reaching Out: A Future for Gratifications Research." In Karl Erik Rosengren, Lawrence A. Wenner, and Philip Palmgreen, eds., *Media Gratifications Research: Current Perspectives,* pp. 255–74. Beverly Hills: Sage.

Bogart, Leo. 1989. *Press and Public,* 2d ed. Hillsdale, N.J.: Erlbaum.

Breed, Warren. 1955. "Social Control in the Newsroom." *Social Forces* 33:326–35.

Brewer, John, and Albert Hunter. 1989. *Multimethod Research.* Newbury Park, Calif.: Sage.

Brody, Richard A., and Benjamin I. Page. 1972. "Comment: The Assessment of Policy Voting." *American Political Science Review* 66(2):450–58.

Broh, C. Anthony. 1973. *Toward a Theory of Issue Voting*. Sage Professional Papers in American Politics. Beverly Hills: Sage.

Brooks, Brian S., George Kennedy, Daryl R. Moen, and Don Ranly. 1985. *News Reporting and Writing*. New York: St. Martin's Press.

Brosius, Hans-Bernd. 1989. "Influence of Presentation Features and News Content on Learning from Television News." *Journal of Broadcasting and Electronic Media* 33(1):1–14.

Brown, Steven R. 1970. "Consistency and the Persistence of Ideology: Some Experimental Results." *Public Opinion Quarterly* 34(Spring):60–68.

Bruner, Jerome. 1990. *Acts of Meaning*. Cambridge: Harvard University Press.

Bryce, James. [1891] 1923. *The American Commonwealth*. New York: Macmillan.

Campbell, Angus, Philip E. Converse, Warren E. Miller, and Donald E. Stokes. 1960. *The American Voter*. New York: Wiley.

———. 1966. *Elections and the Political Order*. New York: Wiley.

Campbell, Deborah C. 1990. "Political Cognition: How Men and Women Understand Issues in the News." Master's thesis, Massachusetts Institute of Technology.

Campbell, Donald T., and Donald W. Fiske. 1959. "Convergent and Discriminant Validation by the Multitrait-Multimethod Matrix." *Psychological Bulletin* 56 (March):81–105.

Campbell, Donald T., and Julian C. Stanley. 1963. *Experimental and Quasi-Experimental Designs for Research*. Chicago: Rand McNally.

Carmines, Edward G., and James A. Stimson. 1980. "The Two Faces of Issue Voting." *American Political Science Review* 74:78–91.

———. 1989. *Issue Evolution: Race and the Transformation of American Politics*. Princeton: Princeton University Press.

Chaffee, S. H., L. S. Ward, and L. P. Tipton. 1970. "Mass Communication and Political Socialization." *Journalism Quarterly* 47 (Winter):647–59.

Chaiken, Shelly, and Alice H. Eagly. 1976. "Communication Modality as a Determinant of Message Persuasiveness and Message Comprehensibility." *Journal of Personality and Social Psychology* 34(4):605–14.

Citrin, Jack, Donald Green, and Beth Reingold. 1987. "The Soundness of Our Structure: Confidence in the Reagan Years." *Public Opinion* 10(4):18–19,59.

Clarke, Peter, and Eric Fredin. 1978. "Newspapers, Television, and Political Reasoning." *Public Opinion Quarterly* 42:143–60.

Clarke, Peter, and F. Gerald Kline. 1974. "Media Effects Reconsidered." *Communication Research* 1(2):224–40.

Cohen, Akiba A. 1976. "Radio vs. TV: The Effect of the Medium." *Journal of Communication* 26 (Spring):29–35.

————, ed. 1989. *Future Directions in Television News Research*. Vol. 33 of *American Behavioral Scientist*.

Cohen, Bernard C. 1963. *The Press and Foreign Policy*. Princeton, N.J.: Princeton University Press.

Cohen, S., and J. Young, eds. 1981. *The Manufacture of News*. London: Constable.

Collins, B. E., J. C. Martin, R. D. Ashmore, and L. Ross. 1973. "Some Dimensions of Internal-External Metaphor in Theories of Personality." *Journal of Personality* 41:471–92.

Collins, W. Andrew. 1982. "Cognitive Processing in Television Viewing." In David Pearl, Lorraine Southilet, and Joyce Lazar, eds., *Television and Behavior: Ten Years of Scientific Progress and Implications for the Eighties*, pp. 9–23. Rockville, Md.: National Institute of Mental Health.

Comstock, George, Steven Chaffee, Natan Katzman, Maxwell McCombs, and Donald Roberts. 1978. *Television and Human Behavior*. New York: Columbia University Press.

Conference on Issues and the Media. *National News Index* (monthly). Arlington, Vir.

Conover, Pamela Johnston, and Stanley Feldman. 1984. "How People Organize the Political World: A Schematic Model." *American Journal of Political Science* 28 (February):95–126.

Converse, Philip. 1964. "The Nature of Belief Systems in Mass Publics." In David Apter, ed., *Ideology and Discontent*. New York: Free Press.

————. 1970. "Attitudes and Non-Attitudes: The Continuation of a Dialogue." In Edward Tufte, ed., *The Quantitative Analysis of Social Problems*, pp. 168–89. Reading, Mass.: Addison-Wesley.

————. 1975. "Public Opinion and Voting Behavior." In F. Greenstein and N. Polsby, eds., *Handbook of Political Science*. Reading, Mass.: Addison-Wesley.

————. 1979. "Rejoinder to Wray." *Journal of Politics* 41:1182–84.

————. 1980. "Rejoinder to Judd and Milburn." *American Sociological Review* 45(4):644–46.

Converse, Philip, and Gregory B. Markus. 1979. "Plus ça change . . . The New CPS Election Study Panel." *American Political Science Review* 73:32–49.

Cook, Thomas D., and Donald T. Campbell. 1979. *Quasi-Experimentation: Design and Analysis Issues for Field Settings*. Chicago: Rand McNally.

Crigler, Ann N. 1986. "Setting the Congressional Agenda: Public Opinion in a Media Age." Ph.D. diss., Massachusetts Institute of Technology.

————, ed. Forthcoming. *Political Communication and Constructing Public Understanding*.

Crigler, Ann N., and Klaus Bruhn Jensen. 1991. "Discourses of Politics: Talking about Public Issues in the United States and Denmark." In Peter Dahlgren and Colin Sparks, eds., *Communication and Citizenship*. London: Routledge.

Crigler, Ann N., Marion Just, and W. Russell Neuman. 1991. "Interpreting Visual vs. Audio Messages in Television News." International Communication Association Annual Conference. Chicago.

Crouse, T. 1973. *The Boys on the Bus*. New York: Ballantine Books.

Curran, James, Michael Gurevitch, and Janet Woollacott, eds. 1977. *Mass Communication and Society*. Newbury Park, Calif.: Sage.

Dahlgren, Peter. 1988. "What's the Meaning of This? Viewers' Plural Sense-Making of TV News." *Media, Culture and Society* 10(3):285–301.

Davis, Dennis K. 1990. "News and Politics." In David L. Swanson and Dan Nimmo, eds., *New Directions in Political Communication: A Resource Book*, pp. 147–84. Newbury Park, Calif.: Sage.

Davis, Dennis K., and John P. Robinson. 1989. "Newsflow and Democratic Society in an Age of Electronic Media." In George Comstock, ed., *Public Communication and Behavior*, 2:60–102. Orlando: Academic Press.

De Fleur, Melvin L., and Sandra Ball-Rokeach. 1988. *Theories of Mass Communication*, 5th ed. New York: Longman.

Delia, Jesse G., and Barbara J. O'Keefe. 1979. "Constructivism: The Development of Communication in Children." In Ellen Wartella, ed., *Children Communicating: Media and Development of Thought, Speech, Understanding*. Newbury Park, Calif.: Sage.

Delli Carpini, Michael X., and Bruce Williams. 1990. "The Method is the Message: Focus Groups as a Means of Examining the Uses of Television in Political Discourse." International Society of Political Psychology. Washington, D.C.

Dennis, Everette E. 1989. *Reshaping the Media: Mass Communication in an Information Age*. Newbury Park, Calif.: Sage.

Diamond, Edwin, and Stephen Bates. 1984. *The Spot: The Rise of Political Advertising on Television*. Cambridge: MIT Press.

Donohew, Lewis, Leonard Tipton, and Roger Haney. 1978. "Analysis of Information-Seeking Strategies." *Journalism Quarterly* 55(Spring):25–31.

Downs, Anthony. 1957. *An Economic Theory of Democracy*. New York: Harper & Row.

———. 1972. "Up and Down with Ecology: The Issue Attention Cycle." *Public Interest* 28:38–50.

Drew, Dan, and Byron Reeves. 1980. "Learning From a Television News Story." *Communication Research* 7:95–120.

Edelman, Murray. 1964. *The Symbolic Uses of Politics*. Urbana: University of Illinois.

———. 1988. *Constructing the Political Spectacle*. Chicago: University of Chicago Press.

Edelstein, Alex S., Youichi Ito, and Hans Mathias Kepplinger. 1989. *Communication and Culture: A Comparative Approach*. New York: Longman.

Edwardson, Mickie, Kurt Kent, and Maeve McConnell. 1985. "Television News Information Gain from Interesting Video vs. Talking Heads." *Journal of Broadcasting* 29(4):367–78.

Elster, Jon, ed. 1986. *Rational Choice*. New York: New York University Press.

Entman, Robert M. 1989. *Democracy without Citizens: Media and the Decay of American Politics*. New York: Oxford University Press.

Epstein, Edward Jay. 1973. *News from Nowhere*. New York: Random House.

Erbring, Lutz, Edie M. Goldenberg, and Arthur H. Miller. 1980. "Front Page News and Real World Cues: A New Look at Agenda-Setting." *American Journal of Political Science* 24:16–49.

Fang, I. E. 1972. *Television News*. New York: Communication Arts.

Ferejohn, John A. 1990. "Information and the Electoral Process." In John A. Ferejohn and James H. Kuklinski, eds., *Information and the Democratic Process*, pp. 1–22. Urbana: University of Illinois Press.

Ferejohn, John A., and James H. Kuklinski, eds. 1990. *Information and the Democratic Process*. Urbana: University of Illinois Press.

Festinger, Leon. 1957. *A Theory of Cognitive Dissonance*. Stanford: Stanford University Press.

Fiorina, Morris P. 1981. *Retrospective Voting in American National Elections*. New Haven: Yale University Press.

———. 1990. "Information and Rationality in Elections." In John A. Ferejohn and James H. Kuklinski, eds., *Information and the Democratic Process*, pp. 329–43. Urbana: University of Illinois Press.

Fiske, Susan, Donald Kinder, and W. M. Larter. 1983. "The Novice and the Expert: Knowledge-Based Strategies in Political Cognition." *Journal of Experimental and Social Psychology* 19:381–400.

Freedman, Jonathan L., and David Sears. 1965. "Selective Exposure." In L. Berkowitz, ed., *Advances in Experimental Social Psychology*, 2:58–98. Orlando: Academic Press.

Frey, Dieter. 1986. "Recent Research on Selective Exposure to Information." In Leonard Berkowitz, ed., *Advances in Experimental Social Psychology*, pp. 41–80. Orlando: Academic Press.

Galtung, Johann, and M. H. Ruge. 1965. "The Structure of Foreign News." *Journal of Peace Research* 2:64–91.

Gamson, William A. 1984. *What's News*. New York: Free Press.

———. 1988. "A Constructionist Approach to Mass Media and Public Opinion." *Symbolic Interaction* 11(2):161–74.

———. 1989. "News as Framing." *American Behavioral Scientist* 33(2):157–61.

———. 1992. *Talking Politics*. New York: Cambridge University Press.

Gamson, William A., and Andre Modigliani. 1989. "Media Discourse and Public Opinion on Nuclear Power: A Constructionist Approach." *American Journal of Sociology* 95:1–37.

Gans, Herbert. 1979. *Deciding What's News*. New York: Pantheon Books.

Gant, Michael, and Dwight F. Davis. 1984. "Mental Economy and Voter Rationality." *Journal of Politics* 46:132–49.

Gardner, Howard. 1981. *The Quest for Mind: Piaget, Levi-Strauss, and the Structuralist Movement*. Chicago: University of Chicago Press.

———. 1985. *The Mind's New Science: A History of the Cognitive Revolution*. New York: Basic Books.

Gerbner, George, ed. 1983. *Ferment in the Field*. Special edition of *Journal of Communication*.

Gerbner, George, Larry Gross, Michael Morgan, and Nancy Signorielli. 1980. "The 'Mainstreaming' of America: Violence Profile No. 11." *Journal of Communication* 30(3):10–29.

Gitlin, Todd. 1980. *The Whole World Is Watching*. Berkeley: University of California Press.

Glasgow University Media Group. 1976. *Bad News*. London: Routledge & Kegan Paul.

———. 1980. *More Bad News*. London: Routledge & Kegan Paul.

Goffman, Erving. 1974. *Frame Analysis*. New York: Harper & Row.

Gollin, Albert E., and Nicolas Bloom. 1985. "Newspapers in American News Habits." New York: Newspaper Advertising Bureau.

Graber, Doris A. 1984. *Mass Media and American Politics*, 2d ed. Washington, D.C.: Congressional Quarterly Press.

———. 1987. "Kind Pictures and Harsh Words: How Television Presents the Candidates." In Kay Lehman Schlozman, ed., *Elections in America*, pp. 115–41. Boston: Unwin Hyman.

———. 1988. *Processing the News: How People Tame the Information Tide*. 2d ed. White Plains: Longman.

———. 1990. "Seeing Is Remembering: How Visuals Contribute to Learning from Television News." *Journal of Communication* 40(3):134–55.

Green, Maury. 1969. *Television News: Anatomy and Process*. Belmont, Calif.: Wadsworth.

Gunter, Barrie. 1987. *Poor Reception: Misunderstanding and Forgetting Broadcast News*. Hillsdale, N.J.: Erlbaum.

Gusfield, Joseph. 1981. *The Culture of Public Problems*. Chicago: University of Chicago Press.

Habermas, Jurgen. 1989 [1962]. *The Structural Transformation of the Public Sphere*. Cambridge: MIT Press.

Hallin, Daniel C. 1985. "The American News Media: A Critical Theory Perspective." In John Forester, ed., *Critical Theory and Public Life*. Cambridge: MIT Press.

Heider, F. 1958. *The Psychology of Interpersonal Relations*. New York: Wiley.

Heilizer, Fred. 1959. "Some Cautions Concerning the Use of Change Scores." *Journal of Clinical Psychology* 15(3):447–49.

Henry, William. 1985. "Television at Its Best." Queenstown, Md.: Aspen Institute.

Hess, Stephen. 1981. *The Washington Reporter*. Washington, D.C.: Brookings Institution.

Hirsch, Paul M. 1977. "Occupational, Organizational, and Institutional Models in Mass Media Research: Toward an Integrated Framework." In Paul M. Hirsch, Peter V. Miller, and F. Gerald Kline, eds., *Strategies for Communication Research*, pp. 13–42. Beverly Hills: Sage.

Hoijer, Birgitta. 1984. "News, Comprehension, and Memory." Ph.D. diss. Uppsala University.

———. 1990. "Studying Viewers' Reception of Television Programmes: Theoretical and Methodological Considerations." *European Journal of Communication* 5(1):29–56.

Hovland, Carl. 1959. "Reconciling Conflicting Results Derived from Experimental and Survey Studies of Attitude Change." *American Psychologist* 14:8–17.

Inglehart, Ronald. 1985. "Aggregate Stability and Individual Level Flux in Mass Belief Systems: The Level of Analysis Paradox." *American Political Science Review* 79:97–116.

Insko, Chester A. 1984. "Balance Theory, the Jordan Paradigm, and the Wiest Tetrahedron." In Leonard Berkowitz, ed., *Advances in Experimental Psychology,* 18:89–140. Orlando: Academic Press.

Iyengar, Shanto. 1991. *Is Anyone Responsible? How Television Frames Political Issues*. Chicago: University of Chicago Press.

Iyengar, Shanto, and Donald R. Kinder. 1987. *News That Matters: Television and American Opinion*. Chicago: University of Chicago Press.

Jamieson, Kathleen Hall. 1988. *Eloquence in an Electronic Age: The Transformation of Political Speechmaking*. New York: Oxford University Press.

Jensen, Klaus Bruhn. 1986. *Making Sense of the News*. Aarhus, Denmark: Aarhus University Press.

———. 1988. "News as Social Resource: A Qualitative Empirical Study of the Reception of Danish Television News." *European Journal of Communication* 3:275–301.

————. 1990. "The Politics of Polysemy: Television News, Everyday Consciousness, and Political Action." *Media Culture & Society* 12(1):57–78.

Jensen, Klaus Bruhn, and Karl Erik Rosengren. 1990. "Five Traditions in Search of the Audience." *European Journal of Communication* 5(2–3): 207–38.

Judd, Charles M., and Michael M. Milburn. 1980. "The Structure of Attitude Systems in the General Public." *American Sociological Review* 45:627–43.

Just, Marion, and Ann Crigler. 1989. "Learning from the News: Experiments in Media, Modality and Reporting about Star Wars." *Political Communication and Persuasion* 6(Winter):109–27.

Just, Marion, Ann Crigler, and Lori Wallach. 1990. "Thirty Seconds or Thirty Minutes: What Viewers Learn from Spot Advertisements and Candidate Debates." *Journal of Communication* 40(3):120–33.

Kahneman, Daniel, Paul Slovic, and Amos Tversky, eds. 1982. *Judgment under Uncertainty.* New York: Cambridge University Press.

Katz, Elihu. 1980. "On Conceptualizing Media Effects." In Thelma McCormack, ed., *Studies in Communications,* pp. 119–41. Greenwich, Conn.: JAI Press.

Katz, Elihu, Jay G. Blumler, and Michael Gurevitch. 1973. "On the Use of the Mass Media for Important Things." *American Sociological Review* 38(2):164–81.

Katz, Elihu, and Paul F. Lazarsfeld. 1955. *Personal Influence: The Part Played by People in the Flow of Communications.* New York: Free Press.

Kelley, Stanley, Jr., and Thad W. Mirer. 1974. "The Simple Act of Voting." *American Political Science Review* 68:572–91.

Kern, Montague. 1989. *Thirty-Second Politics: Political Advertising in the Eighties.* New York: Praeger.

Kessel, John J. 1972. "Comment: The Issues in Issue Voting." *American Political Science Review* 66(2 June):459–65.

Key, V. O., Jr. 1961. *Public Opinion and American Democracy.* New York: Knopf.

————. 1966. *The Responsible Electorate: Rationality in Presidential Voting, 1936–1960.* New York: Vintage.

Kiewiet, D. Roderick. 1983. *Macroeconomics and Micropolitics: The Electoral Effects of Economic Issues.* Chicago: University of Chicago Press.

Kinder, Donald R., and D. Roderick Kiewiet. 1981. "Sociotropic Politics: The American Case." *British Journal of Political Science* 11:129–61.

Kinder, Donald R., and David O. Sears. 1985. "Public Opinion and Political Action." In Gardner Lindzey and Elliot Aronson, eds., *The Handbook of Social Psychology,* pp. 659–741. New York: Random House.

Kiolbassa, Jolene. 1989. "Covering Political Issues: The Closed Loop of Political Communication." Master's thesis, Massachusetts Institute of Technology.

Klapper, Joseph. 1960. *The Effects of Mass Communications*. New York: Free Press.

Kleiber, D., D. J. Veldman, and S. L. Menaker. 1976. "The Multidimensionality of Locus of Control." Eastern Psychological Association. Washington, D.C.

Klingemann, Hans D. 1979. "Ideological Conceptualization and Political Action." In Samuel H. Barnes and Max Kaase, eds., *Political Action: Mass Participation in Five Western Democracies*. Beverly Hills: Sage.

Kornhauser, William. 1959. *The Politics of Mass Society*. New York: Free Press.

Kosicki, Gerald M., and Jack M. McLeod. 1990. "Learning from Political News: Effects of Media Images and Information Processing Strategies." In Sidney Kraus, ed., *Mass Communication and Political Information Processing*, pp. 69–83. Hillsdale, N.J.: Erlbaum.

Kraus, Sidney, and Dennis Davis. 1976. *The Effects of Mass Communication on Political Behavior*. University Park: Pennsylvania State University Press.

Kubey, Robert, and Mihaly Csikszentmihalyi. 1990. *Television and the Quality of Life: How Viewing Shapes Everyday Experience*. Hillsdale, N.J.: Erlbaum.

Ladd, Everett Carll. 1988. "Problems or Voting Issues?" *Public Opinion* 11(2):33–35.

Lakoff, Sanford, and Herbert F. York. 1989. *A Shield in Space: Technology, Politics, and the Strategic Defense Initiative*. Berkeley: University of California Press.

Lane, Robert E. 1962. *Political Ideology*. New York: Free Press.

———. 1973. "Patterns of Political Belief." In Jeanne Knutson, ed., *Handbook of Political Psychology*, pp. 83–116. San Francisco: Jossey-Bass.

Lang, Gladys Engel, and Kurt Lang. 1953. "The Unique Perspective of Television and Its Effect." *American Sociological Review* 18:3–12.

———. 1983. *The Battle for Public Opinion: The President, the Press, and the Polls during Watergate*. New York: Columbia University Press.

Langer, Ellen J. 1989. "Minding Matters: The Consequences of Mindlessness-Mindfulness." In Leonard Berkowitz, ed., *Advances in Experimental Social Psychology*, pp. 137–73. San Diego: Academic Press.

Lanzetta, John T., Denis G. Sullivan, Roger D. Masters, and Gregory J. McHugo. 1985. "Emotional and Cognitive Responses to Televised Images of Political Leaders." In Sidney Kraus and Richard M. Perloff, eds., *Mass Media and Political Thought*, pp. 85–116. Beverly Hills: Sage.

Lau, Richard R., Thad A. Brown, and David O. Sears. 1978. "Self-Interest and Civilians' Attitudes toward the War in Vietnam." *Public Opinion Quarterly* 42:464–83.

Lau, Richard R., and Ralph Erber. 1985. "Political Sophistication: An Information Processing Approach." In Sidney Kraus and Richard M. Perloff, eds., *Mass Media and Political Thought*, pp. 37–64. Newbury Park, Calif.: Sage.

Lau, Richard, and David O. Sears, eds. 1986. *Political Cognition*. Hillsdale, N.J.: Erlbaum.

Lerner, Daniel. 1958. *The Passing of Traditional Society*. New York: Free Press.

Levenson, H. 1973. "Multidimensional Locus of Control in Psychiatric Patients." *Journal of Consulting and Clinical Psychology* 41:397–404.

Levy, Mark R., John P. Robinson, and Dennis K. Davis. 1986. "News Comprehension and the Working Journalist." In John Robinson and Mark Levy, eds., *The Main Source*, pp. 211–28. Beverly Hills: Sage.

Lewis, Carolyn D. 1984. *Reporting for Television*. New York: Columbia University Press.

Liebes, Tamar, and Ann N. Crigler. 1990. "Framing 'Us' and 'Them': Political Discourse in the United States and Israel." International Communications Association Annual Conference. Dublin.

Linz, Daniel, et al. 1991. "Estimating Community Tolerance for Obscenity: The Use of Social Science Evidence." *Public Opinion Quarterly* 55(1):80–112.

Lippmann, Walter. 1925. *The Phantom Public*. New York: Macmillan.

———. 1965 [1922]. *Public Opinion*. New York: Free Press.

Lipset, Seymour Martin. 1985. "Feeling Better: Measuring the Nation's Confidence." *Public Opinion* 8(2):6–9, 56.

Livingstone, Sonia M. 1989. "Interpretive Viewers and Structured Programs: The Implicit Representation of Soap Opera Characters." *Communication Research* 16(1):25–58.

Lowery, Sharon, and Melvin L. De Fleur. 1983. *Milestones in Mass Communication*. New York: Longman.

Luskin, Robert P. 1987. "Measuring Political Sophistication." *American Journal of Political Science* 31:856–99.

MacKuen, Michael B. 1984. "Reality, the Press, and Citizens' Political Agendas." In Charles E. Turner and Elizabeth Martin, eds., *Surveying Subjective Phenomena*, pp. 443–73. New York: Russell Sage Foundation.

Mander, Jerry. 1978. *Four Arguments for the Elimination of Television*. New York: Morrow.

Manheim, Jarol B. 1976. "Can Democracy Survive Television?" *Journal of Communication* 26 (Spring):84–90.

Manoff, Robert Karl. 1989. "Modes of War and Modes of Social Address: The Text of SDI." *Journal of Communicaton* 39(1):59–84.

Manoff, Robert Karl, and Michael Schudson, eds. 1986. *Reading the News.* New York: Pantheon.

Marcus, George E., and Wendy Rahn. 1990. "Emotions and Democratic Politics." In Samuel Long, ed., *Research in Micropolitics,* pp. 29–58. Greenwich, Conn.: JAI Press.

Marcuse, Herbert. 1964. *One-Dimensional Man.* Boston: Beacon Press.

Margolis, Michael. 1977. "From Confusion to Confusion: Issues and the American Voter, 1956–72." *American Political Science Review* 71:31–43.

Markle Commission on the Media and the Electorate. 1989. "Summary Report." New York: Markle Foundation.

Markus, Gregory B., and Philip Converse. 1979. "A Dynamic Simultaneous Equation Model of Electoral Choice." *American Political Science Review* 73:1055–70.

McCombs, Maxwell E. 1981. "The Agenda-Setting Approach." In Dan D. Nimmo and Keith R. Sanders, eds., *Handbook of Political Communication,* pp. 121–40. Newbury Park, Calif.: Sage.

McCombs, Maxwell E., and Donald L. Shaw. 1972. "The Agenda-Setting Function of the Mass Media." *Public Opinion Quarterly* 36:176–87.

McDonald, Daniel G. 1983. "Investigating Assumptions of Media Dependency Research." *Communication Research* 10(4):509–28.

McDougall, C. G. 1968. *Interpretive Reporting.* New York: Macmillan.

McGuire, William J. 1969. "The Nature of Attitudes and Attitude Change." In Gardner Lindzey and Elliot Aronson, eds., *The Handbook of Social Psychology,* 2d ed., pp. 136–314. Reading: Addison-Wesley.

———. 1985. "Attitudes and Attitude Change." In Gardner Lindzey and Elliot Aronson, eds., *The Handbook of Social Psychology,* 3d ed., pp. 233–346. New York: Random House.

———. 1986. "The Myth of Massive Media Impact: Savagings and Salvagings." In George Comstock, ed., *Public Communication and Behavior,* pp. 173–257. Orlando: Academic Press.

McKelvey, Richard D., and Peter C. Ordeshook. 1984. "Rational Expectations in Elections." *Public Choice* 44:61–102.

———. 1990. "Information and Elections: Retrospective Voting and Rational Expectations." In John A. Ferejohn and James H. Kuklinski, eds., *Information and the Democratic Process,* pp. 281–312. Urbana: University of Illinois Press.

McLeod, Jack M., and Lee Becker. 1981. "The Uses and Gratifications Approach to Political Communication Research." In Dan D. Nimmo and Keith R. Sanders, eds., *Handbook of Political Communication.* Beverly Hills: Sage.

McLeod, Jack M., and Byron Reeves. 1980. "On the Nature of Mass Media Effects." In Stephen B. Withey and Ronald P. Abeles, eds., *Television and Social Behavior*, pp. 17–54. Hillsdale, N.J.: Erlbaum.

McLuhan, Marshall. 1964. *Understanding Media*. New York: American Library.

Mencher, Melvin. 1984. *News Reporting and Writing*, 3d ed. New York: Brown.

Meyrowitz, Joshua. 1985. *No Sense of Place: The Impact of Electronic Media on Social Behavior*. New York: Oxford University Press.

Milburn, Michael A., and Anne B. McGrail. 1990. "The Dramatic Presentation of News and its Effects on Cognitive Complexity." Annual Meeting of the American Political Science Association. San Francisco.

Miller, Arthur, Warren E. Miller, Alden Raine, and Thad Brown. 1976. "A Majority Party in Disarray." *American Political Science Review* 70:753–78.

Miller, Warren E., and Teresa E. Levitin. 1976. *Leadership and Change*. Cambridge, Mass.: Winthrop.

Mishler, Elliot G. 1986. *Research Interviewing: Context and Narrative*. Cambridge: Harvard University Press.

Modigliani, Andre, and Franco Modigliani. 1987. "The Growth of the Federal Deficit and the Role of Public Attitudes." *Public Opinion Quarterly* 51(4):459–80.

Nachmias, David, and Chava Nachmias. 1987. *Research Methods in the Social Sciences*. New York: St. Martin's.

Natchez, Peter B. 1985. *Images of Voting/Visions of Democracy*. New York: Basic Books.

Neuman, W. Russell. 1976. "Patterns of Recall among Television News Viewers." *Public Opinion Quarterly* 40:115–23.

———. 1982. "Television and American Culture." *Public Opinion Quarterly* 46:471–87.

———. 1986. *The Paradox of Mass Politics*. Cambridge: Harvard University Press.

———. 1989. "Parallel Content Analysis: Old Paradigms and New Proposals." In George Comstock, ed., *Public Communication and Behavior*, 2:205–89. Orlando: Academic Press.

———. 1991a. *The Future of the Mass Audience*. New York: Cambridge University Press.

———. 1991b. "What Ever Happened to Mass Society Theory?" Annual Meeting of the American Association for Public Opinion Research. Phoenix.

Neuman, W. Russell, and Ann C. Fryling. 1985. "Patterns of Political Cognition: An Exploration of the Public Mind." In Sidney Kraus and Richard

Perloff, eds., *Mass Media and Political Thought*, pp. 223–40. Beverly Hills: Sage.

Neuman, W. Russell, and Ithiel de Sola Pool. 1986. "The Flow of Communications into the Home." In Sandra J. Ball-Rokeach and Muriel Cantor, eds., *Media, Audience, and Social Structure*, pp. 71–86. Beverly Hills: Sage.

Nie, Norman, Sidney Verba, and John R. Petrocik. 1976. *The Changing American Voter,* Cambridge: Harvard University Press.

Nimmo, Dan, and David L. Swanson. 1990. "The Field of Political Communication: Beyond the Voter Persuasion Paradigm." In David L. Swanson and Dan Nimmo, eds., *New Directions in Political Communication: A Resource Book,* pp. 7–47. Newbury Park, Calif.: Sage.

O'Connell, Jacqueline. 1989. "Political Sophistication: An Assessment of Individual Differences across Issues." Master's thesis, Massachusetts Institute of Technology.

Opinion Roundup. 1988a. "AIDS: A Multi-Country Assessment." *Public Opinion* 11(1):36–39.

———. 1988b. "Reagan's Legacy: Defense." *Public Opinion* 10(2):21–28.

Page, Benjamin I., and Robert Y. Shapiro. 1992. *The Rational Public: Fifty Years of Trends in Americans' Policy Preferences.* Chicago: University of Chicago Press.

Paivio, Allan. 1978. "A Dual Coding Approach to Perception and Cognition." In H. L. Lick and Saltzman, eds., *Modes of Perceiving and Processing Information,* pp. 307–33. Hillsdale, N.J.: Erlbaum.

Patterson, Thomas. 1980. *The Mass Media Election: How Americans Choose Their President.* New York: Praeger.

Patterson, Thomas, and Robert D. McClure. 1976. *The Unseeing Eye: The Myth of Television Power in National Elections.* New York: Putnam.

Perloff, Richard M., Ellen A. Wartella, and Lee B. Becker. 1982. "Increasing Learning from TV News." *Journalism Quarterly* 59:83–86.

Perse, Elizabeth M. 1990. "Audience Selectivity and Involvement in the Newer Media Environment." *Communication Research* 17(5):698–715.

Petrocik, John R. 1979. "Level of Issue Voting: The Effect of Candidate-Pairs on Presidential Elections." *American Politics Quarterly* 23:303–27.

Petty, Gary R. 1988. "The Interaction of the Individual's Social Environment, Attention and Interest, and Public Affairs Media Use on Political Knowledge Holding." *Communication Research* 15(3):265–81.

Pierce, John C., and Douglas Rose. 1974. "Nonattitudes and American Public Opinion: The Examination of a Thesis." *American Political Science Review* 68(June):626–49.

Pierce, John C., and John L. Sullivan, eds. 1980. *The Electorate Reconsidered.* Beverly Hills: Sage.

Plato. 1945. *The Republic of Plato*. New York: Oxford University Press.

Polanyi, Livia. 1989. *Telling the American Story: A Structural and Cultural Analysis of Conversational Storytelling*. Cambridge: MIT Press.

Pomper, Gerald M. 1972. "From Confusion to Clarity: Issues and American Voters, 1956–1968." *American Political Science Review* 66(6):415–28.

Popkin, S., J. W. Gorman, G. Phillips, and J. A. Smith. 1976. "Comment: What Have You Done for Me Lately? Toward an Investment Theory of Voting." *American Political Science Review* 70:779–805.

Protess, David L., and Maxwell McCombs, eds. 1991. *Agenda Setting: Readings on Media, Public Opinion and Policymaking*. Hillsdale, N.J.: Erlbaum.

Quester, George. 1990. *The International Politics of Television*. Lexington, Mass.: Lexington Books.

Ranney, Austin. 1983. *Channels of Power: The Impact of Television on American Politics*. New York: Basic Books.

Reese, Stephen D., and M. Mark Miller. 1981. "Political Attitude Holding and Structure: The Effects of Newspaper and Television News." *Communication Research* 8(2):167–87.

Reeves, Ben, Esther Thorson, and Joan Schleuder. 1986. "Attention to Television: Psychological Theories and Chronometric Measures." In Jennings Bryant and Dolf Zillmann, eds., *Perspectives on Media Effects*, pp. 251–79. Hillsdale, N.J.: Erlbaum.

Repass, David E. 1971. "Issue Salience and Party Choice." *American Political Science Review* 65(June):389–400.

Riker, William H., and Peter C. Ordeshook. 1968. "A Theory of the Calculus of Voting." *American Political Science Review* 62:25–42.

Roberts, D. F., and C. M. Bachen. 1981. "Mass Communication Effects." *Annual Review of Psychology* 32:307–56.

Robinson, John P. 1972. "Toward Defining the Functions of Television." In Eli Rubinstein, George Comstock, and John P. Murray, eds., *Television and Social Behavior*, 4:568–603. Washington, D.C.: Government Printing Office.

Robinson, John P., and Dennis K. Davis. 1990. "Television News and the Informed Public: An Information Processing Approach." *Journal of Communication* 40(3):106–19.

Robinson, John, and Mark Levy. 1986. *The Main Source*. Beverly Hills: Sage.

Robinson, Michael J. 1975. "American Political Legitimacy in an Era of Electronic Journalism: Reflections on the Evening News." In Douglas Cater and Richard Adler, eds., *Television as a Social Force*, pp. 97–140. New York: Praeger.

———. 1976. "Public Affairs Television and the Growth of Political Malaise:

The Case of 'The Selling of the Pentagon.'" *American Political Science Review* 70:409–32.

Robinson, Michael J., and Margaret A. Sheehan. 1983. *Over the Wire and on TV: CBS and UPI in Campaign '80*. New York: Russell Sage Foundation.

Rogosa, David, David Brandt, and Michele Zimowski. 1982. "A Growth Curve Approach to Measurement of Change." *Psychological Bulletin* 92(3):726–48.

Rosenberg, Shawn W. 1988. *Reason, Ideology and Politics*. Princeton: Princeton University Press.

Rosenberg, Shawn W., Dana Ward, and Stephen Chilton. 1988. *Political Reasoning and Cognition: A Piagetian View*. Durham, N.C.: Duke University Press.

Rosengren, Karl Erik, Lawrence A. Wenner, and Philip Palmgreen, eds. 1985. *Media Gratifications Research: Current Perspectives*. Beverly Hills: Sage.

Rosenthal, Robert. 1991. *Meta-Analytic Procedures for Social Research*. Newbury Park, Calif.: Sage.

Rothenberg, Randall. 1989. "The Trouble with Mall Interviewing." *New York Times*. August 16.

Rotter, J. B. 1966. "Generalized Expectancies for Internal Versus External Control of Reinforcement." *Psychological Monographs* 80(609):entire.

Rumelhart, D. E., and D. A. Norman. 1985. "Representation in Memory." In R. C. Atkinson, R. J Herrnstein, G. Lindzey, and R. D. Luce, eds., *Handbook of Experimental Psychology*. New York: Wiley.

Salomon, Gavriel. 1979. *Interaction of Media Cognition and Learning*. San Francisco: Jossey Bass.

———. 1984. "Television is 'Easy' and Print is 'Tough': The Differential Investment of Mental Effort in Learning as a Function of Perceptions and Attributions." *Journal of Educational Psychology* 76(4):647–58.

Salomon, Gavriel, and Tamar Leigh. 1984. "Predispositions about Learning from Print and Television." *Journal of Communication* 34(2):119–34.

Schiller, Herbert I. 1989. *Culture, Inc.: The Corporate Takeover of Public Expression*. New York: Oxford University Press.

Schlozman, Kay Lehman, and Sidney Verba. 1979. *Injury to Insult: Unemployment, Class, and Political Participation*. Cambridge: Harvard University Press.

Schroder, Harold M., Michael J. Driver, and Sigfried Streufert. 1967. *Human Information Processing*. New York: Holt, Rinehart & Winston.

Schudson, Michael. 1978. *Discovering the News: A Social History of American Newspapers*. New York: Basic Books.

Sears, David O. 1990. "Symbolic Politics: A Socio-Psychological Analysis."

Annual Meeting of the International Society of Political Psychology. Washington, D.C.

Sears, David O., and Carolyn L. Funk. 1990. "Self-Interest in Americans' Political Opinions" In Jane J. Mansbridge, ed., *Beyond Self-Interest*, pp. 147–70. Chicago: University of Chicago Press.

Sears, David O., Carl P. Hensler, and Leslie K. Speer. 1979. "Whites' Opposition to Busing: Self-Interest or Symbolic Politics?" *American Political Science Review* 73:369–84.

Sears, David O., and Richard R. Lau. 1983. "Inducing Apparently Self-Interested Political Preferences." *American Journal of Political Science* 27:223–52.

Sears, David O., Richard Lau, Tom Tyler, and Harris Allen, Jr. 1980. "Self-Interest vs. Symbolic Politics in Policy Attitudes and Presidential Voting." *American Political Science Review* 74:670–84.

Shapiro, Michael J. 1969. "Rational Political Man: A Synthesis of Economic and Social Psychological Perspectives." *American Political Science Review* 63(December):1106–19.

Shepsle, Kenneth A. 1972. "The Strategy of Ambiguity: Uncertainty and Electoral Competition." *American Political Science Review* 66(June):555–68.

Siebert, Fred S., Theodore Peterson, and Wilbur Schramm. 1956. *Four Theories of the Press*. Urbana: University of Illinois Press.

Sigal, Leon V. 1973. *Reporters and Officials*. Lexington, Mass.: Heath.

Signorielli, Nancy, and Michael Morgan, eds. 1990. *Cultivation Analysis: New Directions in Media Effects Research*. Newbury Park, Calif.: Sage.

Simon, Herbert A. 1985. "Human Nature in Politics: The Dialogue of Psychology with Political Science." *American Political Science Review* 79:293–304.

Smith, Eric R. A. N. 1989. *The Unchanging American Voter*. Berkeley: University of California Press.

Sniderman, Paul M., and Richard A. Brody. 1977. "Coping: The Ethic of Self-Reliance." *American Journal of Political Science* 21:501–21.

Stimson, James A. 1975. "Belief Systems: Constraint, Complexity, and the 1972 Election." *American Journal of Political Science* 19:393–418.

Stokes, Donald E. 1966. "Some Dynamic Elements of Contests for the Presidency." *American Political Science Review* 60:19–28.

Sullivan, John L., James E. Piereson, and George E. Marcus. 1978. "Ideological Constraint in the Mass Public: A Methodological Critique and Some New Findings." *American Journal of Political Science* 22:233–49.

Swanson, David L. 1987. "Gratification Seeking, Media Exposure, and Audience Interpretations: Some Directions for Research." *Journal of Broadcasting and Electronic Media* 31(3):237–54.

Tankard, James W., Jr., Laura Hendrickson, Jackie Silberman, Kris Bliss, and Salma Ghanem. 1991. "Media Frames: Approaches to Conceptualization and Measurement." Association for Education in Journalism and Mass Communication. Boston.

Tichenor, Philip J., George A. Donohue, and Clarice A. Olien. 1970. "Mass Media Flow and Differential Growth in Knowledge." *Public Opinion Quarterly* 34:149–70.

Times Mirror. 1990a. "The American Media: Who Reads, Who Watches, Who Listens, Who Cares?" Washington, D.C.: Times Mirror Center for the People and the Press.

———. 1990b. "The People, the Press, and Politics." Washington, D.C.: Times Mirror Center for the People and the Press.

Tsuneki, Teruo. 1979. *Psychological Experiment on Formats of Information Presentation.* Tokyo: Research Institute of Telecommunication and Economics.

Tuchman, Gaye. 1978. *Making News: A Study in the Construction of Reality.* New York: Free Press.

van Dijk, Teun A. 1988. *News as Discourse.* Hillsdale, N.J.: Erlbaum.

Wartella, Ellen, and Byron Reeves. 1985. "Historical Trends in Research on Children and the Media: 1900–1960." *Journal of Communication* 35(2):118–33.

Wattenberg, Martin P. 1991. *The Rise of Candidate-centered Politics: Presidential Elections of the 1980s.* Cambridge: Harvard University Press.

Weaver, David H., Doris A. Graber, Maxwell McCombs, and Chaim H. Eyal. 1981. *Media Agenda-Setting in a Presidential Election.* New York: Praeger.

Weaver, Paul H. 1975. "Newspaper News and Television News." In Douglas Cater and Richard Adler, eds., *Television as a Social Force,* pp. 81–96. New York: Praeger.

Weiss, W. 1968. "Effects of Mass Media Communication." In G. Lindzey and E. Aronson, eds., *Handbook of Social Psychology,* pp. 77–195. Reading, Mass.: Addison-Wesley.

Woodall, W. Gill, Dennis K. Davis, and Haluk Sahin. 1983. "From the Boob Tube to the Black Box: TV News Comprehension from an Information Processing Perspective." *Journal of Broadcasting* 27(2):173–93.

Worchel, S., V. Andreoli, and J. Eason. 1975. "Is the Medium the Message? A Study of the Effects of Media, Communicator and Message Characteristics on Attitude Change." *Journal of Applied Social Psychology* 5:157–72.

Wright, Charles R. 1974. "Functional Analysis and Mass Communication Revisited." In J. G. Blumler and E. Katz, eds., *The Uses of Mass Communication: Current Perspectives on Gratifications Research,* pp. 197–212. Newbury Park, Calif.: Sage.

Zaller, John. 1992. *Political Competition and Public Opinion*. New York: Cambridge University Press.

Zukin, Cliff. 1981. "Mass Communication and Public Opinion." In Dan D. Nimmo and Keith R. Sanders, eds., *Handbook of Political Communication*, pp. 359–90. Beverly Hills: Sage.

Zukin, Cliff, and Robin Snyder. 1984. "Passive Learning: When the Media Environment Is the Message." *Public Opinion Quarterly* 48:629–39.

Index

172 INDEX

television hypothesis, 10–11, 40, 48–
51, 80–87, 113, 122, 144n
television superiority hypothesis, 78–80,
143n; complementarity of television
with other media, 93; success of television with low salience topics, 113;
visual excitement in presentation and
learning benefits, 78–79, 92
Thorson, Esther, 79
three-element model, 19. *See also* constructionism
Tichenor, Philip J., 101
Time, 31, 34, 37, 47, 72, 136
Times Mirror News Interest Index, 2, 34,
41–42, *42–43*
Tipton, Leonard, 98, 109
Tsuneki, Teruo, 79
Tuchfarber, Alfred J., 141n
Tuchman, Gaye, 5, 37, 60, 111, 119
Tversky, Amos, 15
Tyler, Tom, 15

uninformed voter theory, 7, 12–14, 16,
96, 98–99, *98*, 141n
Union of Concerned Scientists, 46
United States, 62, 65–66
University of Michigan, 47
USA Today, 115
U.S. Drug Enforcement Agency, 47
uses and gratifications perspective, 108
U.S. News and World Report, 31

Vanderbilt Television Archives, 50–51,
50

van der Voort, Tom H. A., 85
van Dijk, Teun A., 5, 60–61, 80, 142n
Veldman, D. J., 143n
Verba, Sidney, 13, 15, 40, 141n
Vietnam, 40
voter participation in the United States,
xv. *See also* political disengagement in
democracies

Wallach, Lori, 58
Ward, Dama, 27
Ward, L. S., 98
Waring, H. Ross, 11
Wartella, Ellen, 15, 48–49
Washington Post, 30
Wattenberg, Martin P., 11
Weaver, David H., 10
Weaver, Paul H., 49
Weiss, Walter , 9
Wenner, Lawrence A., 11, 17
West Bank, 40
Whitney, D. Charles, 11–12
Woodall, W. Gill, 108–109
Woolacott, Janet, 9
Worchel, S., 18
Wright, Charles, 79

York, Herbert F., 45–46
Young, J., 60

Zaller, John, 141n
Zimowski, Michele, 81
Zukin, Cliff, 3